Thoughts on life and Advertising

Thoughts on life and Advertising

To Kitt Sullivan,

One of the family!

Best wishes,

Hugh Salmon

Xmas '19

Hugh Salmon

Copyright © 2016 Hugh Salmon

The moral right of the author has been asserted.

Apart from any fair dealing for the purposes of research or private study, or criticism or review, as permitted under the Copyright, Designs and Patents Act 1988, this publication may only be reproduced, stored or transmitted, in any form or by any means, with the prior permission in writing of the publishers, or in the case of reprographic reproduction in accordance with the terms of licences issued by the Copyright Licensing Agency. Enquiries concerning reproduction outside those terms should be sent to the publishers.

Matador
9 Priory Business Park,
Wistow Road, Kibworth Beauchamp,
Leicestershire. LE8 0RX
Tel: 0116 279 2299
Email: books@troubador.co.uk
Web: www.troubador.co.uk/matador
Twitter: @matadorbooks

ISBN 978 1785891 304

British Library Cataloguing in Publication Data.
A catalogue record for this book is available from the British Library.

Printed and bound by CPI Group (UK) Ltd, Croydon, CR0 4YY
Typeset in 11pt Aldine401 BT by Troubador Publishing Ltd, Leicester, UK

Matador is an imprint of Troubador Publishing Ltd

*To the memory of my mother,
who died the day I finished this project.*

CONTENTS

Introduction   X

1. YOU
1.1. What makes you special?   3
1.2. Someone really special   5
1.3. The need to know who you are   7

2. YOUR LIFE
2.1. Ability. Application. Attitude. Three As for a successful career   11
2.2. When you don't know what you don't know   13
2.3. Seve Ballesteros and Richard Branson's dad   15
2.4. Don't make your hobby your job   17
2.5. A job that's forever not just for life   20
2.6. Do you have to be two-faced to succeed?   22

3. LIFE AND DEATH
3.1. Work. Partner. Home. Three decisions in life you have to get right   27
3.2. James Hunt: enjoy life while you can   31
3.3. A human insight to stop kids smoking in the first place   35
3.4. When a human right is a human wrong   38
3.5. The right to die   39
3.6. You can't practise pressure   42
3.7. A tribute to my father   44

4. LEADERSHIP
4.1. Leadership: Be Driven. Be Smart. Be Human.   49
4.2. The Queen – Never complain. Never explain.   52
4.3. Richard Branson – Flexibility is the Key   54

4.4. When you need someone to do something they don't want to do	56
4.5. A master class in the art of chairing a meeting	58
4.6. The Pope's opportunity to overcome vested interests in Christianity	61
4.7. What Sir Alex Ferguson could learn from David Ogilvy	66

5. ADVERTISING

5.1. It may be right. It may be good. But is it interesting?	71
5.2. Strategic thinking: some people don't get it, do they?	74
5.3. Strategic thinking: be decisive but keep an open mind	76
5.4. How the UK Government ignored the most basic law of advertising	78
5.5. Man's inhumanity to man	81

6. MARKETING

6.1. Marketing = consumers = customers = cash	87
6.2. Branding: understanding the importance of trust	90
6.3. The difference between a commodity and a brand	92
6.4. The difference between a product and a service	95
6.5. The human importance of customer service (1)	99
6.6. The human importance of customer service (2)	101
6.7. Books: 'Form is temporary. Class is permanent.'	103

7. OFFICE POLITICS

7.1. The affliction of intellectuals who see all sides of an argument	107
7.2. The better you do, the worse it gets	110
7.3. When, even if you are right, you are wrong	111
7.4. When your greatest strength is your greatest weakness	113

8. SPORT

8.1. When all you can do is play the ball bowled to you	117
8.2. Digital media, rugby and gutless management	121
8.3. What politicians could learn from rugby (and the Marines)	123
8.4. Being English, British and European in sport	125

9. MUSIC & POETRY

9.1. If you can whistle, you're not tone deaf	129
9.2. The way forward for rock bands	131
9.3. Why you would be a mug to be a poet	134

10. MEDIA

10.1. Super-injunctions, contra mundum orders and social media	139
10.2. How the Beeb blew it	143
10.3. Humanity can overcome technology	146
10.4. Digital fish fight drives democracy	148
10.5. Mourning Big Brother and exposure of social prejudice	151
10.6. The perverse cult of celebrity	153

11. RANDOM CONSUMER INSIGHTS

11.1. A breath of fresh air for health clubs and gyms	159
11.2. Retail search (not)	161
11.3. Privacy in-store and out	164
11.4. Halfords bicycle chase	166
11.5. Marks & Spencer – a customer insight	168
11.6. What's in a name?	169
11.7. Galaxy chocolate makes the book world sick	172

12. DO AS YOU WOULD BE DONE BY

12.1. Kindness? That takes effort	179
12.2. Crossing the road	181
12.3. Car horns – what for?	182
12.4. Please don't blow that whistle!	185
12.5. Do you brighten the space you occupy?	187

13. APPENDIX – BLOWING THE WHISTLE

13.1. Whistleblowers – brave heroes or social outcasts?	191
13.2. The whistleblower's dilemma – what would YOU do?	194
13.3. Whistleblowing – a call for new legislation	197

Acknowledgements	200

INTRODUCTION

9 JANUARY 2015

In my day, if you wanted to go to Oxford or Cambridge, you had to stay at school for an extra term – and do a hell of a lot more work. My trouble was that the extra term was the rugby term. Whether this is an excuse for my failure, the fact is I failed.

I was puzzled by this. I hadn't failed at anything else, so how could Oxbridge not want me now? After all, as well as the rugby, I had been captain of the school cricket team and, although the grades weren't great, I had achieved five A levels. And my school must have thought I was clever enough as they put my name down in the first place. Surely there had been a mistake? Sadly not.

My father told me I had not taken my studies seriously enough. He questioned my academic commitment wherever I went to university. If anything, he thought I would work even less hard as sex and drinking would be allowed, and drugs available.

I agreed with my dad so, from the ages of 18-22, I lived the life in London. I was a car cleaner, a car dealer, a delivery driver and an accountant. I spent the summer of 1979 teaching water-skiing in Corfu.

Then I got lucky.

By the same age as my contemporaries, who had taken the academic high road, I knew I wanted to be an adman. I had friends at Ogilvy & Mather (O&M) and Foote, Cone & Belding (FCB). Both offered me jobs as a graduate trainee. I chose O&M.

Two years later, I told my boss about my idea for a music magazine on cassette tape. He loved the idea and asked me if he could help. I said I needed offices, so SFX was launched just along the corridor.

SFX was a great ride but, sadly, we ran out of money and I returned to advertising, as an Account Director at FCB and a Board Director at Kirkwoods. Then in 1988, when I was 31, Ogilvy got me back to manage the Thailand office, their fourth largest in the world (and possibly their best). After that, and having got married and had our first child, Ogilvy transferred me back to London to oversee the Unilever account.

Then I got unlucky.

The American I was to replace in Ogilvy London announced she would not be going back to New York after all. The job Ogilvy had transferred me back to London to do wasn't there any more. Instead, they wanted me to manage the Middle East region out in Bahrain. But my wife and I did not want to live in Bahrain. And, by this time, I had been approached by Lintas, another Unilever agency, to manage CM:Lintas with a promise this would lead to my heading up all the Lintas operations in London.

Soon after arriving at CM:Lintas in 1992, I found the Chairman was defrauding the company by diverting money into a personal account elsewhere. He was a crook. I tried to persuade him to stop. He tried to fire me. I reported him to head office. They did fire me. Worse, to cover up the fraud, they told lies about me which I felt affected my reputation in the advertising industry.

This led to a five year litigation in which I wanted to clear my name. I had no idea it would take so long. In 1997, I won the case in 'spectacular' fashion. An executive of Interpublic Group, holding company of Lintas Worldwide, and quoted on the New York Stock Exchange, flew over to London on Concorde, issued a public statement effectively admitting the fraud, made a fulsome apology and paid me £475,000 damages.

In taking on this litigation, I feared I may never work in a multinational advertising agency again and this has turned out to be the case. After two years as Managing Director of a small London advertising agency, I established The Salmon Agency in 1999. Soon after this, I began to suffer chronic back pain from an old rugby injury and in time, after four operations, found the active life of managing a business difficult to sustain.

So I started to write as, back in the day, my teachers had thought I could do.

In the hands of the NHS, I have witnessed the suffering some people are forced to endure and I began to feel that the understanding of human behaviour and the creative talent I had worked with, in advertising, could be better applied to improving the lives of the unlucky people in the world.

From 2009-15, a full 'parliamentary period' if you like, I wrote the blog 'A Different Hat' on BrandRepublic.com. I have had no vested interests to protect, no selfish cause to promote. Just a naïve hope that, one day, something I have written might make someone else's life better.

I have re-ordered my posts from the chronological order in which they were published to the subject matter to which they relate. In this way, I do hope that, in here somewhere, there is something that might make your life a little better too.

I have divided my 'blog books' into two:

1. 'Thoughts on Life and Advertising' is based on my own working life.

2. 'Ideas for Britain' is an ebook which deals with society on a wider, more political, level.

I hope you enjoy reading them.

Hugh Salmon

1
YOU

1.1. WHAT MAKES YOU SPECIAL?

25 MAY 2012 08:52

Last night, I watched a TV programme called Safari Vet School with my teenage daughter. The show features a group of young vets helping to protect endangered animal species in a South African game reserve.

Whatever panics and dangers they faced, the local Head Vet, Dr Will Fowlds, exuded an extraordinary air of calm professionalism. At the end of the two weeks, he took them for a moment's quiet reflection overlooking miles of unspoilt, distant African landscape.

'This view has been here all my life. And it was here, one day, that I realised something very important and I hope you have learnt too: it is very difficult to interact with people around you or achieve your full potential until you understand who you are and what your weaknesses are; what you are good at and what you are special at.'

These words reminded me of a Memorial Service I attended some years ago to celebrate the life of a man who had taught my father Maths in the 1930s and me in the 1970s. Mr Wort.

Eulogies were given by former pupils from the 1940s, the 1950s and the 1960s. It is this last one I remember most. It went something like this:

"The months before I met Mr Wort had been the most worrying in my life. For it had been announced, at the beginning of the summer holidays, that, at the end of the summer holidays, my father would drive me from our home in the West Country to my new boarding school nearer London.

This was a terrifying prospect. In my whole life, I had never really spoken to my father and the thought of sharing a four-hour car journey with him filled me with fear.

The day came and, after three and a half hours of stone cold silence in our rickety old car, I felt I should say something. After all, this was mid-

September and I wouldn't be seeing my father until Christmas. Surely we should talk?

So I asked my father a question. I admit it was a stupid question for not only did I know the answer, but I knew he knew I knew the answer. I asked him:

'Father, did you go to this school?'

'Of course I did', he replied.

More silence.

As we drove through the school gates and unloaded my bags from the car, still quivering with fear, there was one question I thought I really must ask my father before saying goodbye:

'Father, did you enjoy it here?'

'Of course not. It was a dreadful place', he replied and drove back to Devon.

At this point, Mr Wort came up to me, put his arm round my shoulders and said:

'Hello, young man. Welcome to your new school. Tell me, what are you good at? Maths? English? Art? Music? Sport?'

'I'm not good at anything, sir.'

'Oh yes you are. I have been at this school for many years and I know there is something you are good at, something that makes you special. In fact, I have a feeling there is something you are better at than anyone else in this school, if not the whole of England. You may not know it now – and it may not be what you expect it to be – but, over the next five years, it is my job to find out what it is. Will you help me?'

I knew then I had made a friend for life. And I am honoured to pay tribute to Mr Wort today."

So am I.

1.2. Someone Really Special

30 April 2012 08:57

So, in my last post, we were talking about my old teacher's conviction that everyone is special at something. It brought to mind a story a friend of mine told me about his brother.

I met Tom Wilson through cricket. He is friendly, sociable and gregarious. Good player too. The story he told me was about his brother, Robert, about whom his family were extremely concerned.

Robert didn't like cricket (which is certainly a concern). In fact, he didn't like any sport at all. He didn't like reading. He didn't like music. He didn't like art. He didn't like pubs. Robert didn't like anything. He just sat in his room all day looking at the ceiling. It was a struggle for the family to coax him downstairs to eat or watch TV.

For his twenty-first birthday, Robert's godfather gave him a present – an expensive, extensive personality assessment and career guidance course.

Robert was asked to complete various forms and answer penetrative personal questions. He was interrogated by a psychologist. He was analysed by an analyst. He was invited to practise the art of conversation. He was monitored in social situations. He was even watched secretly through a two-way mirror having a meal with a group of carefully selected friends and family.

He was taken apart.

At the end of the week, he was summoned by the head honcho to receive his verdict.

'Mr Wilson, we have assessed you and your character from every angle. We have watched you. We have talked to you. Unfortunately, we have not been able to listen to you because, quite frankly, you have nothing to say. You are without doubt the most boring, lifeless, insignificant person we have ever had on this course.'

Tears formed behind Robert's glasses, trickled down his cheeks and dropped onto his creased, ill-fitting trousers. No one has felt more useless.

'You don't care about other people. You never ask them questions. You show no interest in their lives. You never look them in the eye. You are completely unobtrusive. No one notices you in a room. No one even remembers you have been there. You are a total nobody.'

As his shoulders collapsed and his heart bled, Robert's tears turned to sobs and he drew from his pocket a grotty, grey handkerchief which he wiped across his face and smeared over his misted glasses.

And these are the perfect qualities for a private detective.

Robert looked up. And he smiled. And, now, this is what he does. And he is very successful.

For Robert is a very special person.

With a very special talent.

1.3. THE NEED TO KNOW WHO YOU ARE

12 MARCH 2013 09:01

Last week, I heard Jeffrey Archer promoting his latest book on the radio.

In the light of Chris Huhne's jail sentence for perverting the course of justice, the presenter insisted on asking Archer about his own experiences in prison. Monosyllabic were the answers. Not quite the PR His Lordship was after.

Isn't it odd how some people take for granted an outstanding talent they possess in sacrifice of a dream they are never going to achieve?

They just don't know, or won't accept, what they are good at.

It seems Jeffrey Archer is one of these. A convicted perjurer, and thus a proven liar, he may have thought this an ideal talent for political office – but, to his considerable cost and with plenty of time for reflection in jail – he may now accept that telling lies is more suitable for an author of fiction than a respectable public figure.

I went on a cricket tour to Australia with a person like this. Let's call him Ned.

Ned was completely deluded as to his cricketing talent and, however quickly he thought he could bowl, he wasn't slow in telling the rest of us, time after time and day after day, what a famous and successful international player he would become (not).

As so often, the more Ned talked the less we believed him – to the extent that, back home in England, he decided to become a professional golfer instead (not).

However, Ned did have one talent which we all admired. He was a wonderful magician. After every game, he would work his magic on the opposition (far more than he had on the pitch) and they would be spellbound by his talent – as were we, his teammates.

My favourite of Ned's tricks was when he would pretend he couldn't find the playing card his victim had picked from the pack, only to find it in someone's pocket. And then, to the surprise of all, in another pocket he would find the victim's watch, which none of us had seen him remove.

If you have never seen a magician close-up and in person, it is much more impressive than on stage or TV. This guy was good – and certainly not what you expect in a clubhouse bar in the middle of Australia after a long, hot game of cricket, I can tell you.

Why couldn't Ned recognise, and realise, his own talents? Strange, isn't it?

When advising students on their career options, I ask them if, whatever academic qualifications they may have or whatever subjects they may have studied, they have a mind which can compete with other people with more relevant skills in their chosen career.

What does this mean?

Well, early in life, I discovered something about the way my own mind works.

Compared to some people, I am very weak at remembering lists of facts. This, I like to fool myself, leaves space in my brain for the unequalled brilliance of my human insights and creative thinking.

Over a beer in a pub, I would meet friends with jobs in The City who could remember accurately the closing price of every share on the London Stock Exchange. Would you put money on being able to do this?

Or, I would dine with people who could not only recognise a wine variety, which I can just about do, but also the vintner and vintage. 'Oh, that's a Chateau Plonk 1983' say they, leaving me feeling embarrassed and socially inadequate.

Even more annoyingly, I know people who can remember every racehorse in the country, where it has run before and its place in the race. This knowledge helps them win money off innocent punters like me who haven't a clue.

I know I would never have succeeded as a stockbroker, a wine merchant or a gambler.

But can such people communicate?

That's another story.

2
YOUR LIFE

2.1. Ability. Application. Attitude. Three As for a successful career

15 August 2013 09:04

Good luck to students who receive their A Level results today. If you have achieved your aims, good on you. If not, please do not despair. The longer you live, the less important they will be.

Take it from me, the exam results you achieve at school are no criteria for a successful career.

When I achieved a level of management where people began to ask me for careers advice or – far harder – to review or appraise my colleagues' performance, I wanted to recommend books to help them improve themselves and their prospects. After all, what is the point of criticising anyone without offering guidance on how to progress? And what better guidance than a book?

This was when I became aware of how little my A Levels had prepared me for management or, for that matter, a life in business at all. In particular I recognised with guilt, and no little horror, that I had read pathetically few textbooks on career success or business management – subjects in which I was now supposed to be an expert. Indeed, so little had I read that I could never catch up.

The more I found out, the less I knew.

So, modest as ever, I developed Hugh Salmon's Three 'A's for A Successful Career by which I could impart my words of wisdom while covering up my own ignorance. Here they are:

1. Ability

Never in your career should you be challenged to understand anything you are not capable of understanding. If you are, you are in the wrong business. With all honesty, I can say that never in my career have I been asked to do this (having said that, I have just read Sweet

Tooth by Ian McEwan and did struggle a bit with The Monty Hall Problem).

Choose a career which fits your Ability. Only you know what that is.

And, as you well know, your Ability is not defined by your A Levels. They are no indicator of your character, creativity, charisma, charm or even your cooking or your cricket – all of which lie within your natural Ability and can be far more important than academic achievement.

By the way, you can be too clever: The affliction of intellectuals who see all sides of an argument. And be careful. However smart you think you are there is always someone smarter than you.

2. Application

Application is not just a test of hard work, although all successful people do work hard. The most important test of your intelligence is how intelligently you Apply it to your Ability. Your success in doing this is likely to define how successful you will be.

It is vital that you make career choices that fit your character. The more you enjoy your work, the more you will Apply yourself to it.

By the way, there's another key point under Application. You will face set-backs. We all do. When this happens, don't go off track. Apply yourself. KBO. Keep Buggering On.

3. Attitude

When I managed Ogilvy Thailand, we had 400 people in the office. But, frankly, when it came to the big presentations, particularly to our multinational clients, it was down to me. It was what I was paid to do. I had the A Levels.

Yet, the Thais were great people to work with. Nothing was too much trouble. They didn't push back. They bounced back. And they always came back smiling. This is Attitude.

By the way, when I returned to London to work with the biggest A★ brains in the business – first class degrees from Oxbridge; the lot – I heard about lovers who were hated, spouses who had left home, children in prison (oh yes), drink and drug addictions. What negativity. What hard work!

Please don't sink this low. Just remember:

Ability. Application. Attitude.

The only 'A's anyone will ever need.

2.2. When you don't know what you don't know

16 July 2012 08:46

Sir Nicholas Hytner, has directed 'The History Boys', 'Warhorse', 'One Man Two Guv'nors' and more at the National Theatre. He understands how people think and act. In a recent TV profile, he said this about acting:

'The ones who make it are the ones who know how little they know.'

Past and present colleagues will read this and smile for, in business and in life, the following has been a recurring mantra of mine:

'You know what you know. You know what you don't know. But what if you don't know what you don't know?'

Famously, this time to bewildered laughter, the former United States Secretary of Defence Donald Rumsfeld tried to explain this mantra in simple terms – but only made it more complicated for his audience (and won himself a 'Foot In Mouth' Award):

'There are known knowns – there are things we know that we know. There are known unknowns – that is to say there are things that we now know we don't know. But there are also unknown unknowns – there are things we do not know we don't know.'

So what did Sir Nicholas Hytner mean by 'the ones who make it are the ones who know how little they know'? As so often, flip the argument and you find the answer. Clearly, Hytner was saying that the actors who think they know it all (when they don't) will not succeed – whereas actors who are willing to learn, will.

On a business level, companies that fail to continually ask questions about every aspect of their business model run the risk of attack from innovative new competitors. A topical example is the book market where a number of established publishing houses have failed to see the potential in downloadable ebooks such as 'Fifty Shades of Grey'.

On a wider level, a more worrying social characteristic has emerged.

Take the media. It seems a greater than average proportion of television presenters and journalists have parents in the same sector.

Why is this? It is not necessarily the case, as some might think, that the parents have pulled strings to secure glamorous jobs for their children. No, these parents have had the advantage of knowing what their children do not know and been able to set them on a path of learning that children with parents from outside the media have not been able to identify.

Because they do not know what they do not know, 'outsiders' find it difficult to break in, thus giving the children of those already in the sector an unfair advantage.

Nepotism is alive and well in society today.

Don't you just know it.

2.3. SEVE BALLESTEROS AND RICHARD BRANSON'S DAD

27 JUNE 2011 08:03

I never have enough time to read.

Often, I find myself scanning the newspaper without the time to read articles that I really want to read – and concentrate on reading.

One example is obituaries. I hate not reading about the lives of people whom I have admired and respected – and I love reading about the lives of people about whom I knew nothing but whose lives, on reading about them, I find fascinating.

So, by my favourite armchair at home, there builds a steady pile of unread material. Sometimes these pages are there for so long they go sepia in the sun.

Yesterday, on the sunniest day of the year, she who must be obeyed ordered me to work my way through this ageing and unsightly pile – or she would throw it away.

Then a strange thing happened. As Jung would have said, synchronicity occurred.

As long ago as 9 May, I had kept the obituary of Severiano Ballesteros. What talent. (I admire talent).

Then, just as I finished reading about Seve (most of which I knew but might never read again), my eyes were drawn to a photo of Richard Branson and his father, Edward Branson.

I have met Richard Branson a couple of times and enjoyed doing so. And I thought it might be interesting to read about his father (about whom I knew nothing).

I learned that Edward Branson had wanted to be an archaeologist, but his own father had insisted that he prepare for a career in the law.

Later, Branson père would recall a similar exchange between himself and his son:

"There was a time when I felt Richard ought to get a qualification, so I walked him up and down our lawn at home and said I would like him to qualify as a barrister.

Later, I felt awful because I had said to him just what my father had said to me. So, the next weekend, I walked him up and down the lawn once again and told him to forget everything I'd said." Respect.

This reminded me of something I had just read about Seve, one of the most naturally talented golfers ever to have played the game. I returned to his obituary:

"Practice was carried out in the family's barn, in which he would drive the balls again and again into a hanging backcloth. He later said that between the ages of 12 and 18 he had probably driven as many as 1,000 golf balls a day."

So, there you go, two men – one born in 1918 and the other in 1957 – whose obituaries were published on exactly the same day in 2011, come together to give all the career advice anyone needs now and forever:

DO WHAT YOU LIKE AND WORK YOUR BALLS OFF!

Then, in the immortal words of Arthur Daley, the world is your lobster.

2.4. DON'T MAKE YOUR HOBBY YOUR JOB

1 FEBRUARY 2012 08:27

Yes, yes, yes! At last! The day has arrived. In the long history of the Internet, I can only post this blog on this one day. Yes, today. 1 February 2012.

'One-two. One-two'. 'One-two. One-two'. That's it. Today. 1.2.12. 'One-two. One-two'. 'One-two. One-two'.

I don't know about today's generation, but what a resonant phrase for mine. 'One-two. One-two'. 'One-two. One-two'. Rock and roll!

The audience is buzzing. The lights are down. The stage in gloom. Out of the darkness, a guitar note twangs. A drum rolls. 'One-two. One-two'. 'One-two. One-two'. The roadie tests the mic. Or should that be the 'mike'? Certainly not the mick.

The audience applaud, whistle, cheer. Backstage, the band loosen up and draw that final drag. 'One-two. One-two'. 'One-two. One-two'.

Louder now, and more excited, the audience noise builds in anticipation. Excitement. Expectancy. 'One-two. One-two'. 'One-two. One-two'.

On come the lights, multi-coloured, moving and bright. The drummer, already seated, fires out a louder, longer drum roll. The bassist, tall, long-legged, thin, lopes onto the stage and, fag in mouth, loops his guitar strap over his shoulder. The spotlights wave around the arena until they point to the rest of the band, whose random tuning syncs into a recognisable tune. The singer leaps out from stage right, charges to the microphone and throws himself into his signature track.

The gig is on. The music loud. The audience out of control. One huge, smoky, roomful of human togetherness. Great days. Great memories.

They started at school where, unbelievable now, Genesis came down and played in our small, rickety, pre-war theatre. Pete Gabriel had broken his leg leaping off stage the week before (as you do). He was stuck in a chair but, even so, still a vibrating, electrified chaos of thrashing arms and legs. Then came Hawkwind. And the immortal Edgar Broughton Band. 'Out, demons, out! Out, demons, out!' Rebellion! Rock and roll!

When my pal George and I made it to the VI Form, we felt the baton pushed into our hands. And we grabbed it. We called Chrysalis and booked Pink Fairies. Out with the fairies, more like. They turned up stoned, stayed stoned and tripped meaninglessly around in an introverted whirl of psychedelic nonsense. Just like them, we didn't have a clue, but it wasn't cool to admit that. We were hip.

The next term, we got UFO. 'Doctor, doctor, please. The state I'm in!' We booked them. We met them. We knew them. We were there, man!

Then, later, only a few short years later, with the arrival of the Sony Walkman and the sudden ubiquity of audio cassettes, and working for respectable, civil service Ogilvy & Mather London, I had the idea that music magazines like the NME and Melody Maker would be better expressed in cutting-edge audio format than tired old newsprint.

All of a sudden, I was in the music business. SFX was born. The upside was great. The excitement of the early business plans. Finding the best, the very best, music writer in London. Cosying up to the music companies and their ad agencies with the excitement of our innovative new idea. I had my photo taken by Anton Corbijn. U2? Me too.

Ogilvy, brilliantly, let us offices. Snazzy, red-carpeted Reception welcomed Echo and The Bunnymen, Aswad, The Eurythmics, Paula Yates, Jools Holland and Pete Tong alongside the Marketing Directors of American Express, Shell and Unilever. Madness.

'Outside' meetings were at EMI, Virgin, Chrysalis and Island. So cool.

But do you know what? Over time, the more I got to know the business behind the music business, the less I liked it. More sportsman than junkie, I prepared carefully-thought-through, professional presentations to stoned, out-of-their heads Marketing Directors. A non-smoker, I went to gigs where I could hardly see anyone for the smoke or understand them for what they had smoked. Out of bright lights and glamour, disillusion seeped into my soul. It just didn't feel right. I was out of place. It wasn't me.

And the more it went on, the less I liked it. And the less I liked it, the less motivated I felt. Yet it had been my idea. My baby. Friends had bought into it and left their jobs to join in. But I just didn't have the music in me any more. I lost my mojo.

2.4. DON'T MAKE YOUR HOBBY YOUR JOB

Now, later in my career, I meet youngsters, fresh out of Uni, keen to make the most of their lives. And so many say to me 'I am sporty. I want to work in sports marketing'. Or 'I like food. I want to own a restaurant'. Or 'I'm into music. I want to be in the music business'.

And I think 'No! Please – no! Don't do it. Don't risk the loss of that which you love. Don't make your leisure your business. Don't make your hobby your job.'

Because if you do this, and you become disillusioned, you may find you have sacrificed the freedom to enjoy that which you most enjoy – unencumbered by commerce, unminding of the P&L and not caring of the financial consequences. And you may never enjoy that freedom again.

Perversely, Jimmy Goldsmith's mantra comes to mind: 'Don't marry your mistress. All you do is create a vacancy.' But there's a different moral to that story.

In the meantime, roll on 12 December, when this post will mean something in America.

2.5. A JOB THAT'S FOREVER NOT JUST FOR LIFE

22 June 2012 08:29

This week, anyone who's anyone in advertising has been basking in sunny Cannes at the International Advertising Festival.

As no one knows what advertising is anymore, which is not great advertising for advertising, the Festival is now called the International Festival of Creativity.

Take it from me, as I've been there done that, this is a very expensive occasion which may or may not be appropriate in these austere times.

More positively, these awards will transform some people's lives. I love it when a totally-unheard-of person from a totally unexpected country wins a Grand Prix or a Lion d'Or (sic).

Me? I am here in rainy London, where I have been asked to help a handful of graduates decide their career options. Why me?

It surprises me that so many 'kids' approach this vital decision on a quantitative level. 'I took these A Levels and got this degree so I thought I should be an accountant.'

But what are you like? What sort of person are you? Who do you like being with? Are you a hard worker? Do you like to work on your own? Or function best in a team? What tasks do you enjoy? What do you find a bore? What motivates you? What are your hobbies? What books do you love reading? Oh, you don't?

Once we have discussed these qualitative matters, we are closer to the career choices on offer (or not). Sometimes these kids and their parents are surprised about the range of options available to them – though not many are as special as the 'really special' person I decribed earlier (see 1.2).

For me, I made a very early decision that I wanted a career that would pay me money for things I enjoyed doing, not just earning money for its own sake. This little personal insight counted out a lot of alternatives to the advertising choice I am glad I made.

2.5. A JOB THAT'S FOREVER NOT JUST FOR LIFE

I also liked the idea that some of my work would live forever. Something creative, something tangible, something I could show my family and leave to my kids when my deadline comes. A professional legacy, if you like.

I would have liked to have been Graham Greene. He wrote two sides of A4 before breakfast every morning and spent the rest of his day at leisure. But, as I do not have his talent, and will not earn his royalties, I take pleasure in showing these graduates the work I have done in my career so far.

No, they don't always find this as boring as spreadsheets. Even if they do, it gives me a good insight into their personality which is something neither they or their parents seem to have studied.

In the meantime, back in sunny Cannes, some very talented people have been presented with Awards that no one can ever take away from them and may live forever. Each award will define their working lives – and make them some money too.

I think that's brilliant.

2.6. Do you have to be two-faced to succeed?

14 JUNE 2011 08:15

Hypocrisy – 'the practice of claiming to have more noble standards than is the case'.

This week, I have been thinking about people at each end of their careers, the more worrying of which I will come to later.

First, our universities have started breaking up (sic) and parents have asked me to meet four students so as to advise them on whether marketing or marketing services might be an appropriate career move for their little darlings.

Either that or, faced with a summer of having them back at home (the 'boomerang generation'), the parents just want their kids to get out of the house and do something – even if it is just come and see me.

I've done quite a bit of this over the years and have enjoyed the subsequent career success of some of my ex-protégés (blimey, my PC is more acute than I thought).

In fact, I have some basic rules of engagement which I am now going to make public (and thereby negate their efficacy. Hey-ho).

We usually meet in a bar. This 'equalises' the meeting and helps the youngster feel that this is a chat with a mate rather than any sort of formal interview (although two such meetings have turned into job offers for vacancies I didn't even know I had).

It also tests how serious they are.

If they just want a beer and a chat, then fine – that's what they get. I like meeting young people. It helps me feel young too.

If they turn up with pen and paper or, these days, an electronic gadget, to take notes then I assume they are serious and I try and give serious advice.

If they have Googled me, looked up my website, discovered my own background and are interested in some of the things I have done,

2.6. DO YOU HAVE TO BE TWO-FACED TO SUCCEED?

then I think they are polite as well as serious. Further, because they have shown an interest in me, I am interested in them and maybe I can provide personal as well as professional advice (more later).

If they ask me to look at their CVs but haven't done either of the above, then I don't bother. They aren't going to take note of what I say anyway.

If they have explored the business, found out how it works, pinpointed the role they want to fill and worked out why they think they are a perfect fit then sometimes I can help.

By the way, at one time in my agency, when we were actually recruiting grads, I asked this guy if he knew the difference between creative and account management and he replied: 'I was hoping you would tell me that'. That's not a good line.

I always ask students to think not just of what they want to do (or their parents want them to do) but the sort of people they enjoy being with and the environment in which they feel most comfortable in (do they enjoy working alone or with other people?) – emotional as well as rational or, if you like, qualitative and quantitative.

Until now, it has seemed to me that you are most likely to be successful if you are happy in what you do.

Then, last week, I found myself watching the cricket at Lord's with someone from the marketing services sector whom I have known for the whole of my career.

We were talking about the world facing kids leaving universities these days and something I had read about our generation being the first in history to leave our kids facing a harsher world than that of the generation before them.

And our conversation moved on to the other end of the spectrum.

What has happened to people who, having started with all the ambition, hope and enthusiasm every one of us had at the beginning of our careers, which of us have made it big-time, who have plateaued (yes, that is a word) and who – I am afraid – have lost out altogether and hit upon hard times?

My companion and I now know who these people are. We can identify them.

He then said something that truly shocked me (I paraphrase):

"In my experience most of the people who have made it big-time (i.e. millions) – not all of them but most of them – live completely double lives.

When they go to work, they behave ruthlessly and viciously to achieve their goals. They give not one jot for the people they work with or who work for them. They are completely single-minded on their own success.

And then, when they go home, they are pussies. They play happy families. They have romantic dinners with their other halves. They take the kids out at weekends. They are all chummy with their neighbours and the parents from their kids' schools. They volunteer for this and that. All is rosy. Domestic bliss. But I know that, underneath all that, they are complete and utter shits".

So here we are.

I am about to meet all these bright young things and try to help them find a career which will bring them eternal wealth and happiness and all the excitement that life has to offer.

But what approach should I take?

Is my 'qualitative and quantitative' counsel wise?

Or should I advise them that, if they want to succeed, they should be completely and utterly ruthless (devious if necessary). They should choose a profession where they are least likely to make personal friends with people in the office, keep their working lives completely separate from their home lives, pretend to be nice while doing whatever it takes to stuff people over – and be prepared for this to happen to them?

Is this how it is?

3
LIFE AND DEATH

3.1. Work. Partner. Home. Three decisions in life you have to get right

30 August 2013 09:02

In life there comes a time when, like me, you've had more than you've got left.

When this happens, you can look back at decisions you – and your contemporaries – have got right (and, I'm afraid, wrong).

In my experience, you have only three decisions that are really important:

1. Work

You have to find a sphere of work that depends not only on your academic qualifications but which suits your character as well as your ability:

If you find a job that suits you, you are more likely to be good at it.
If you are good at what you do, you are more likely to enjoy it.
If you enjoy what you do, you are more likely to work hard at it.
If you work hard at what you do, you are more likely to succeed.
It's not rocket science is it?

If, as you read this, you are unhappy at work, please bear in mind that I do not mean a particular business or company but a sphere of work – a sector.

For example, for a time, I found myself in the music business. I like music. Music rocks. But I did not enjoy the music business: 'Don't make your hobby your job'.

2. Partner

Most of us like to share our lives with someone we love. It doesn't matter what sex they are, where they are from, what colour they are or even, as long as they are over 16, how old they are. These things are of no concern to anyone else but you. It is your decision. Yours to get right. Yours to get wrong.

Several years ago, a very close friend of mine called me. He said I was the only person in the world he could talk to. He had met a girl he was thinking of marrying. What did I think?

I was worried. If my friend married this girl, I was sure he wouldn't be happy. I also knew that if I told him this and he ignored my advice, he would be bound to tell his wife – as partners do – and I would lose a friend.

So what did I say?

Well, do you remember the times when you wake up in the morning and you wish you had said something the night before but you didn't and now you can't?

Luckily, on this rare occasion, I said what I wanted to say when I needed to say it. I told my friend that, going in to the arrangement, marriage is something you have to be 100% sure about. Not 95%, not even 90%. Any gaps, I said, will only get wider. From the start you need to be 100% sure.

What happened?

My friend said he was 65% sure and proposed the following week!

He said all his friends were getting married and it was time he did too. Huh?

Another friend of mine got engaged to a woman who had a dark secret. I knew what it was but her fiancé, my friend, did not.

What happened?

I told him. He married her. Then he divorced her. I didn't see my friend for the entire duration of this marriage and his now ex-wife has wrought misery and confusion on my friend and their children ever since.

A third person I know, at work the day after his honeymoon, had lunch with a lady he did not know I was seeing at the time. When she asked him how his honeymoon had been, he said he wished it had been her who he married. Huh?

Difficult things, marriages. And worth getting right.

Mind you, I once sat next to a recruitment consultant at a dinner party. She revealed that her company had developed some bespoke software that defined the optimum characteristics required by candidates in her business sector.

3.1. WORK. PARTNER. HOME. THREE DECISIONS

The computer model showed it to be a positive benefit to have had a failed marriage. In her eyes, putting your career before your marriage should be regarded as a strength.

Isn't that awful? Not, I thought, a lady who would ever help me find a job.

What happened?

She hasn't!

3. Home

Where you live may seem an easy decision – but it can be harder to get right than you think.

Soon after breaking into advertising, I realised that, if I was to live in the UK, I had to work in London. Yes, there are provincial advertising agencies but they have never had much influence and that is what they are. Provincial.

One day, I was talking about this to an art director I worked with. He was from Rotherham. One day, he said, he wanted to go home and live near his family. He wanted his parents to spend time with his children. But he had identified the problem. He could not build a successful career in advertising and live in Rotherham. He now lives in Australia. Not very close to Rotherham. Or his family. Poor guy.

When I worked in Thailand, I realised expat life was not for me. For other expats, Bangkok had irresistible attractions. It didn't matter what sex they were, where they were from or what colour they were – and some of them, I'm appalled to say, were under 16 years old.

But these 'attractions' did not interest me. I love my wife. I like London. My employers talked about opportunities in Korea, New Zealand, Chile and Canada. Not very near home.

Eventually, I was offered a posting back in London. On arrival in the office, the promises that had been made to me were broken and my life had polarised. Either I stayed with my company but lived abroad. Or I stayed in London and left my job at a company I loved.

What happened?

As I like living in London, and don't respect people who break their promises, I left.

By the way, however successful you are at work, you need to consider whether your partner is happy at home. You have a responsibility for his or her wellbeing as well as your own.

And sometimes it can be easier to go somewhere than it is to come back:

Work.

Partner.

Home.

The three decisions in life you just have to get right.

3.2. JAMES HUNT: ENJOY LIFE WHILE YOU CAN

13 SEPTEMBER 2013 09:06

Twice in the last week, I have watched Rush the new film about Niki Lauda and James Hunt.

James was the first 'celebrity' I ever met. As a schoolboy in the 1970s, not only did I meet him – but he drove me in his car!

Well, not his car but, thankfully, a hire car.

In the passenger seat was another Grand Prix driver called Jody Scheckter. I was in the back with one of James's younger brothers, a close friend of mine at school.

This was after a Grand Prix at the Nürburgring in Germany when, after the race, we needed to get to a train station. James said he was going our way and would give us a lift.

And, boy, what a lift it was!

Let's just say that James became a little bored with the spectator traffic leaving the circuit and decided to take what we might call – er – an alternative route.

I won't say any more. All I can do is urge you to go and see 'Rush'. Albeit with Niki driving, the guys in the back of the car after the brilliantly observed hitchhiking scene could have been me.

My other memory of that exhilarating journey was a conversation I had had with the late Harvey Postlethwaite, the designer of James's Hesketh Formula One car. It went something like this:

'Hi Hugh. I hear James and Jody are giving you a lift to the station.'

'Yes Doc.'

'Do you realise what Jody has done today?'

'No Doc.'

'He crashed head on into a barrier at 180mph. Do you have any appreciation how fast that is?'

'No Doc.'

'It's the same as two trains each travelling at 90mph, crashing – smack! – head on and you are one of the drivers two feet from the point of impact. That's what happened to Jody three hours ago. And now he is walking about as if nothing had happened. These guys are something else.'

And he was right.

As a story, if there is one thing 'Rush' gets right it is the proximity to death that Formula One drivers faced at the time. In the opening scene of the film, Niki Lauda voices over that, by the end of any given season, two of the twenty or so drivers would be dead.

These days, it is hard to comprehend how unsafe Formula One motor racing was thirty years ago:

The man who waved the chequered flag stood in the middle of the track as the cars sped past; petrol tanks were refilled by jugs splashing into a funnel; photographers lay on the grass verge of the circuit and nonentities like me – me for goodness sake! – wandered around the pits with lightweight T-shirts down to our navels, ridiculous flared jeans and flip-flops.

For the drivers, death was a constant reality. In checking facts for this post (i.e. getting my years right) here are some lines that emerge from just two races at the Nürburgring:

'Howden Ganley suffered a serious accident … his legs were dangling out the front of the car. He managed to get out by himself but he collapsed, his ankles seriously injured. This led to Ganley's retirement from Formula 1.' (1974)

'Mike Hailwood was another to crash, having a large accident at Pflanzgarten in his McLaren M23. He received a badly broken leg which became a career-ending injury.' (1974)

'Ian Ashley had an accident at Pflanzgarten and suffered serious ankle injuries.' (1975)

'Lauda passed Tom Pryce, who had fuel leaking into his cockpit (!) and could not drive at race pace.' (1975)

Two weeks after the 1975 race at Nürburgring, I found myself at the Österreichring near Salzburg for the Austrian Grand Prix.

This was the scene of the comic incident when Italian driver Vittorio Brambilla, so overjoyed at his first and only Grand Prix win, shot past us on the finishing straight waving both his hands in the air in celebration.

3.2. JAMES HUNT: ENJOY LIFE WHILE YOU CAN

So exuberant was the Gorilla that he forgot to keep at least one hand on the steering wheel in order to turn the corner at the end of the straight. His car smashed head on into the barrier, condemning the joyful Brambilla to the ignominy of completing the only lap of honour in his F1 career with a big ego but a broken nose cone.

Oh sorry, did I say this was a 'comic incident'?

I haven't told you the American driver Mark Donohue crashed at the same corner the day before. And died.

'Rush' brilliantly conveys what have now been shown to be these completely unnecessary dangers that were prevalent in motor racing at the time, particularly Niki Lauda's near fatal accident at the Nürburgring in 1976 – the year after I was there.

Faced, every season, with a high chance of dying, these drivers reacted in different ways. As history, and 'Rush', portray it:

- Niki Lauda was the clinical Austrian who worked hard to minimise the risks he was taking.

- James Hunt was the glamorous playboy who indulged himself in wine, women and smokes.

The truth is that neither of these human characteristics are as clear cut as you might expect:

- Niki Lauda knew how to enjoy himself

- James, as I can testify, was a perfectly sensible and intelligent person who was absolutely dedicated to, and totally serious about, his motor racing career

And they were both great drivers. World Champions. Quick.

In advertising, we have a thing called 'tone of voice' by which creative teams are briefed to convey the personality of the brands we promote.

Well, let me tell you, when James Hunt walked into a room, everyone knew it. The mood lifted. Everyone smiled. People laughed. The tone of voice, as we would have it, became 'fun, enthusiastic, joyful, positive, inclusive, sharing, social with a hint of jealousy and expectation. Vibrant. Irresistible.'

James was the most charismatic person I have ever met. As a world champion in a dangerous, murderous sport he was as alive as anyone could be.

In this sense, he changed my life.

In 1993, after his sudden death of a heart attack aged 45, I sat at his memorial service, feeling desperately sorry for his young sons, and realised James had left me a lesson in life.

I have not had the talent, the opportunities or, frankly, the money he enjoyed.

But, if I had not known James Hunt, I may not have taken my stand against financial corruption at Interpublic, or been to The Bahamas so often, or started my own business, or stood for Parliament, or founded a successful rugby club, or become Trustee of a charity, or published a children's book, or taken my family to New Zealand to experience the Millenium before you did, or flown to Sydney for the World Spoofing Championship, or co-founded Lovereading.co.uk, or written a film script, or worked with so many clients on such a variety of projects, or seen so much of my children, or churned out so many of these infernal blog posts!

In short, I may have had a more successful career – but would I have enjoyed such a full life?

I think you know the answer.

Thank you James.
You're a star.
RIP.

3.3. A HUMAN INSIGHT TO STOP KIDS SMOKING IN THE FIRST PLACE

8 JULY 2010 22:14

I'm sticking with the 'insight' theme for now. After all, this is what 'A Different Hat' has promised from the start (eyes right).

I am really annoyed that people, particularly young people, still smoke cigarettes.

I can understand why it is difficult to stop smoking once you have got the habit. But how and why do people start smoking in the first place?

Unless I've missed something, the vuvuzillions of pounds that have been spent on campaigns to stop people smoking have missed the key insight that lies behind their taking up this anti-social, unhealthy and expensive habit in the first place.

All the campaigns I've seen have been based, in one way or another, on 'fear'.

Blackened lungs, body beating, people dying, coffins, funerals, formaldehyde, fatty stuff, clogged arteries, premature ageing, mouth cancer, throat cancer, lung cancer, passive cancer, inherited cancer ('I like what you like'). Kill yourself. Kill your kids.

For years now, even as a non-smoker, I have seen these campaigns and I have become increasingly annoyed. I'm sick to death of them.

Don't these people get it?

There are two jobs here:

1. Persuade people who are already hooked on smoking to stop smoking.

2. Stop them starting.

I understand that the best way to persuade people who are already hooked may be to remind them constantly of the harm they are doing to themselves, even showing their cheeks being pulled by sharp, pointed fish-hooks (hooked, fish-hook, geddit?).

I suspect, however, that the smokers who are hooked are well aware of the dangers. They have made a conscious decision that this is something they enjoy and they are damn well going to do it.

Thus, in a rather perverse way, these messages of fear merely feed the rebellious devil inside that poked them into smoking in the first place and reinforce their decision to carry on regardless. They're happy where they are.

Which gets me to stopping people starting, a particular concern of mine as my kids are of an age where I suspect they may be about to cross this dangerous threshold.

And the reason I am annoyed about all these campaigns, and the unjustifiable waste of public and charity money they have wasted, is that telling the kids that this will be an unhealthy habit to hook into is the last thing that is going to stop them.

"Aw, Dad, I'll give up after school. Don't be so boring. Everyone does it".

"Aw, Dad, I know I said I would give up after school but I'll give up after Uni. All my friends do it. And you are SO boring."

So here's the insight.

Kids start smoking because they think it is cool. It is a show of independence. They have to be one of the gang. This is imperative. One of the gang, they cannot not be. For kids of a certain age, I cannot tell you how important this is.

I would stake my life on this insight (or smoke with, apparently, the same effect).

So, the best reason I can think of to persuade my kids not to smoke is to spin this thing and convince them that the coolest thing to do is actually not to smoke – that the rebellion is to rebel against the rebellion.

Smoking is not cool. It is the opposite of cool. I do not have the words to define this. If this was the 1960s, 'square' might have done it but, in this sense, square became square and is no longer in the vernacular – nor is it a strong enough word anyway.

But I do think this would be a great brief for more talented people than me:

"Create a social environment where people who smoke cigarettes are perceived by the rest of society, especially the coolest of cool kids, that smoking is totally uncool".

If this could be achieved, the kids would be united and they would never be divided from their own kids, later in life, by dying of lung cancer.

3.3. A HUMAN INSIGHT TO STOP KIDS SMOKING

That's the insight.

Finally, by way of a fag end, I have the right to contradict myself. This week we have been asked by Messrs Clegg and Cameron to propose laws we would like repealed. Well, if some pubs and restaurants want to be 'Smokers Allowed', then I think they should have this right. If smokers want a fag in these pubs or restaurants, then I do not think it is the Role of Government to tell them not to.

I just won't be going there (which is why other pubs and restaurants, the majority I hope, will choose to stick to their current, non-smoking and much cooler position).

3.4. WHEN A HUMAN RIGHT IS A HUMAN WRONG

24 JULY 2012 23:49

Sitting, lounging, reading books – as I am now – by a swimming pool overlooking the Mediterranean Sea, it is natural to absorb more sunshine than news. But the full horror of the Denver Dark Knight killings has penetrated this tranquil state and destroyed the lives of hundreds of innocent people, oceans away from here.

No doubt thousands of commentators have written millions of pages about this crime (not many of which, frankly, have I read).

But how many people were reading – as I was last week – the seminal American novel 'Freedom', by Jonathan Franzen, on the very day the news from Denver came through? In the book, Franzen writes this:

'It's all circling round the same problem of personal liberties ... even if your kids are getting shot down by maniacs with assault rifles ... Bill Clinton figured out that we can't win elections by running against personal liberties. Especially not against guns.'

Creepy, huh?

I am sure much comment has been made in defence of America's gun laws but I would like to contribute one small thought – and I am sorry if you have read this elsewhere.

What about the protection that the victims of these Denver killings were entitled to?

Is protection not a role of government, a civil liberty, a human right?

Over the Olympic period, and in this Presidential election year, I wonder if, every time the American national anthem celebrates 'The Land of the Free', there will be hundreds of victims in Denver and billions of people around the world thinking 'oh no, you are not'.

3.5. THE RIGHT TO DIE

21 JUNE 2011 08:11

Undoubtedly the most thought-provoking and much discussed media event last week was Sir Terry Pratchett's BBC documentary 'Choosing to Die'.

In 1978, a friend of mine called Roger broke his neck in a motor racing accident at Brands Hatch. In those less enlightened days, a race-track marshal rushed to the scene of the accident and yanked Roger's helmet off, severing his spinal column and condemning him to life as a tetraplegic (paralysed from the neck down).

Every week, I went to see him at the Stoke Mandeville Hospital. Once he realised the finality of his condition, we discussed whether his life would be worth living.

In those days, the form was for an able-bodied person such as me to somehow get hold of a cyanide pill, then place it on the tetraplegic's tongue and leave the room – the theory being that, as he would be alone when he swallowed the pill, it would have been his decision to end his life.

As he couldn't move any other part of his body, how else could he kill himself?

This issue was dramatised in the stage play 'Whose Life Is It Anyway' by Brian Clark. By some creepy coincidence, it was being performed in the West End at around the same time as Roger's accident. I watched the brilliant Tom Conti in the lead role.

Sir Terry Pratchett's programme brought back all the issues I try not to think of.

For those who missed it, it showed the voluntary, dignified death of motor neurone disease sufferer Peter Smedley at the Dignitas Clinic in Switzerland. By the way, if you want this post to have more relevance to our industry, then I do think that 'Dignitas' is a brilliant brand name – because, it seems to me, 'dignity' gets right to the heart of this issue.

Also last week, a lady called Helen Cowie from Glasgow called BBC Radio Scotland. She admitted she had helped her son Robert kill himself at Dignitas after he, too, was paralysed from the neck down. Robert chose to die to the Oasis song Listen Up.

The police are looking into the circumstances of this death.

In the UK, Mrs Cowie has broken the law. 'I would rather have been able to do it in this country' said the grief-stricken mother.

My own sympathies are with her.

However, as Dr James Le Fanu said:

'It is only sensible to keep in mind the contrary arguments.

Ninety-year-old Margaret White articulated the first in a recent letter to a newspaper, observing that while she was more than happy living in her nursing home with no wish to die, "were voluntary euthanasia to be legalised I would feel it my duty to ask for it as I now have 19 descendants who need my legacy".

Then there is the invidious position for severely physically disabled people; in a recent survey of those afflicted with cerebral palsy, nearly three quarters were concerned that any changes in the law in favour of assisted dying would create pressure to end their lives prematurely.

For these and others, the flip side to the human right to assisted dying might too readily become an oppressive social obligation.'

For once, there is nothing any research, any sophisticated strategic planning or any brilliant creative can do to find and define a clear – and right – answer.

There are, it seems to me, no right and no wrong answers.

But should it be a matter for the law?

Is it the Role of Government to deny you the right to kill yourself?

All I can tell you is that if you are at all interested in the human condition and humanity at the extreme of its emotional and rational intelligence, then:

- catch the Sir Terry Pratchett programme ('Choosing to Die')

- watch the film 'Whose Life Is It Anyway' (with Richard Dreyfus in the lead role)

- and read 'Still Me' by Christopher Reeve (whose riding accident injured him to the same extent as someone who was hanged at the gallows in less human days)

3.5. THE RIGHT TO DIE

By the way, over 30 years after his accident, Roger still lives in a Cheshire Home.

He paints with his mouth. How creatively brave is that?

Let me know if you would like to buy one of his paintings. Better still, go and see him in the Tunbridge Wells Seven Springs Cheshire Home and choose from his portfolio.

I have one of his paintings framed in the hall of my house.

Talk about a reality check.

I cannot begin to understand the thoughts and emotions Roger has had to live with.

And, finally, next time you want to shout at a work colleague (or your computer), just be grateful that this is not all you can do.

3.6. You Can't Practise Pressure

29 June 2012 08:33

In the European Cup this week, the England v Italy quarter final and the Spain v Portugal semi-final have been decided by penalty kicks in which a player is asked to put the ball on a spot and kick it past a goalkeeper into a goal (or not).

In this way, rather than a contest of skill, the 'game' becomes more of a mental ordeal whereby the penalties continue until one player cracks under pressure and fails to score.

Players have 'choked' in other sports too. In his book 'Bounce', Matthew Syed explored the theory that all you need is up to 10,000 hours practice to reach a level where the motor mechanisms in your body become automatic.

Surely, when under pressure to perform in an environment and atmosphere that you simply cannot practise, you need to think smarter too?

I am no footballer, but I wonder how many of these players, when faced with a level of pressure that they cannot possibly practise, have really thought through what might happen? Are they mentally, as well as physically, prepared? To me, it seems not.

In my own life, I can remember two occasions when I have felt under a pressure I could not practise.

The first was when WPP bought Ogilvy at the time I was managing the Thailand office. Soon after the takeover, Sir Martin Sorrell and his team swept round the Asian offices and I, as a relatively young ad man, was faced with a nerve-wracking presentation to one of the sharpest financial brains in the world.

I remember going home the night before. The presentation was fixed. I knew all my words. But what was this guy going to ask me? What hadn't I thought of? Where were the holes?

3.6. YOU CAN'T PRACTISE PRESSURE

Luckily, I pinpointed three potential questions, two of which were thrown at me by Sir Martin. Without hesitation, I looked him in the eye and gave him my answers.

I passed the test (I wasn't fired).

The other time was when I read the eulogy at my father's funeral, the hardest thing I have been asked to do. The night before, I tried to think through all the things that might happen other than my failing to keep emotional control.

What, for example, would I do if someone's telephone went off at my most emotionally vulnerable moment?

Well that's exactly what happened. And I had my answer:

'If that's Dad, please tell him I miss him.'

3.7. A TRIBUTE TO MY FATHER

12 May 2012 08:45

My dad died ten years ago. As the eldest of his four sons, it fell upon me to give the eulogy at his funeral – the hardest job I have ever done.

You are unlikely to have direct interest in my father as a person but there are two facets of his character, and his life, that you might care to consider.

How many of today's leaders would have volunteered to rebate all income earned outside their salaried job back to their employers, to the extent that by the time of his retirement my father's employers were 'earning' more from him than they were paying to him?

If you have anti-colonial feelings, please consider the possibility that a great many British 'expats' were good people who made a positive contribution to the people and communities they lived with and in. I am proud to say my dad was one of them. I hope you agree:

"He was born on 27 September 1921. In 1940, after only one term at Oxford, he was called up to the army. By the end of the War, he was a Captain and had served in India, Egypt, Persia, Lebanon, Singapore and India again.

After the War, in England but not wanting to go back to Oxford, as a 25 year old and after five years fighting a war, he accepted a job in Calcutta (Kolcata) with Mackinnon Mackenzie, the Far Eastern agents of the P&O shipping company.

Soon, he was transferred to Malaya, where he lived in Penang for three years. And then to Japan, where he lived in Kobe for three and a half years.

In 1954, he was posted to Hong Kong. In 1963, he was promoted to Chairman and Managing Director of Mackinnon Mackenzie Hong Kong and there began 10 happy years.

3.7. A TRIBUTE TO MY FATHER

Professionally, this was his most fulfilling period. Apart from his day job with the P&O, he was Chairman of Mackinnon's Godown, Pennell & Company, Sworn Measurers and Weighers Ltd, Travel Tours Ltd, Shanghai Dockyards and the Hong Kong Electric Company.

He was a Director of the Hong Kong & Shanghai Bank, Mercantile Bank, Union Insurance Society of Canton, Dairy Farm, Hong Kong Tramways, Indo China Steam Navigation Ltd, Union Waterboat Company, Star Ferry, Hong Kong Wharf Company, Douglas Steamship Company, Taikoo Dockyards and Cathay Pacific Airways.

After he retired he revealed to me that, apart from his basic Mackinnons salary, any or all of the fees generated from these directorships were sent back to the P&O in London. He just felt this was the right thing to do.

There were also public appointments. These directly involved him in the Government of the colony. He was a member of the Legislative Council, where he sat on the Finance Committee, the Public Works Committee and School Fees Committee.

Unusually, for a period, he sat on both the Legislative Council and the Executive Council, effectively The Cabinet, at the same time.

He was a member of the Hong Kong Trade Development Council, the Hong Kong Tourist Board, the Port Committee, the Court of the University of Hong Kong and the Tenancy Tribunal. He was appointed a Justice of the Peace in 1968.

There was also voluntary work with the Hong Kong Chamber of Commerce, the Far East Freight Conference, the Federation of Hong Kong Industries, the Joint Associations Committee on Employer/ Employee Relations, the Chinese Language Committee, the Festival of Hong Kong Committee, the Hong Kong Chinese University Committee, Outward Bound, and the Cheshire Homes.

In 1973, he was awarded the OBE for services to the community in Hong Kong.

But I believe it is not what he did in his life that set my father apart, but the way he did it. How he behaved. He was friendly, considerate and courteous. He had a nice word, and a smile, for everybody.

He was modest and completely unmaterialistic. He valued the simple things in life, some of which in his later years, and to his great sadness, were denied him: golf, gardening, bridge, his health and even, at the end, his speech.

He believed in doing the right thing and doing things the right way, even when he knew that doing the right thing would not be easy, or the consequences difficult to face.

He was a man of the world but, more importantly, he was a man of his word. He was absolutely honest. When he said he would do something, he did it. He meant what he said.

And, sometimes, we have to admit, he said what he meant: even if this gave the impression that he could be a little tactless, a little strong-willed, a little stubborn. (Remarkably, none of his four sons have inherited these characteristics!).

Above all, he was enormous fun. In fact, he was probably more fun to be with, and more fondly thought of, than he himself realised. He had a ready smile, a twinkle in his eye, and a healthy sense of the ridiculous, particularly if he felt people were being pompous or taking themselves too seriously.

He was witty, he was warm and he was wise. And he was wonderful company.

There is one final thing I would like to say.

If anyone in this church, or who knew my father at all, ever has a difficult decision in your life, or a personal dilemma, I would urge you to pour yourself a large whisky, or, if it is before lunch, a pink gin; sit down in your favourite armchair; look up from the crossword; look away from the Test Match on the telly; look out through your drawing room window into the garden; and say to yourself: 'What would Gerry Salmon have done?'

Because, if you do this, I know that your decision will be the right one, that you will be a better person, and that he won't have died at all."

4

LEADERSHIP

4.1. Leadership: Be Driven. Be Smart. Be Human.

7 November 2011 08:45

I have been thinking about 'Leadership' as a topic for this post. What a nightmare.

The thought occurred with wry amusement that the 'Leadership for a Better Britain' theme at the Conservative Party Conference was followed, within days, by the biggest back-bench rebellion Cameron has faced as Prime Minister.

Then I started researching Leadership as a topic.

How naïve was that?

Leadership is all over the place, especially online.

There is so much Leadership on Twitter that it becomes impossible to follow. There are Leadership Quotes and Arts of Leadership and The Leadership Mystique and, for all I know, Leadership of Leadership.

I entered 'Leadership' into an Amazon Book Search and 71,064 results appeared. That is a big readership and a lot of Leadership!

Where is all this Leadership leading?

How much Leadership can we take?

How much Leadership do we need?

I don't want to write the 71,065th book on Leadership so here are my Insights on Leadership based on my own commercial experience.

The Leaders I have met fall into three categories:

1. Driven

Driven Leaders are a force of nature. They accomplish more in a day than most people do in a week. They never stop. You can reach them any time of day or night, year after year. They are relentless.

Their sheer drive and energy makes it impossible to argue with them or divert them from their own chosen path. You do what they want you to do because otherwise you would not be working with them. There is no other way.

You are comfortable to work with them because, inside yourself, whatever you think and whatever you feel about these Leaders, you know you could never keep up. Secretly, you so admire their sheer drive and energy that you accept your role is to follow in their wake.

I am not naming names but I guess anyone who is anyone in marketing and marketing services can think of one outstanding example of this type.

2. Smart

Smart Leaders are hard to define. It is unlikely they are academic achievers. They may not even think much about what they do, but they have instinct.

I met Felix Dennis. I can't link you to the Sunday Times Rich List because of their perverse paywall, but here is the Birmingham Post version. He's worth £550million.

The first time I met Felix, he said: 'You're not going to show me a presentation are you? I don't want it. Have a cup of tea. Sit down. You know your business. Tell me about it. Talk to me'.

So I did. Then he proceeded to dissect our business and the market sector with such insight and precision that everything he said has emerged to be true two years later. It would be inappropriate to reveal the details.

But I can share one great anecdote. Felix Dennis said words to this effect:

'You see these magazines on the shelf behind me? They have made me very rich. But I can tell you that all the kids leaving university these days want to go into digital. They think that is the future. But do you know how the richest man in Britain, the sixth richest man in the world made his money? Steel. F*****G STEEL!'

Forbes says Lakshmi Mittal is worth $431.1billion. Made of steel. I think that's funny.

Earlier in his career, maybe Felix was driven as well as smart. Not now. He lives in Mustique, is planting a forest in Warwickshire and lives a balanced life. That's smart.

4.1. LEADERSHIP: BE DRIVEN. BE SMART. BE HUMAN.

It is possible to be Driven and Smart. If so, you are really rocking. From what I have read, Steve Jobs was like this. RIP.

But, the question has been asked, was he a kind person?

3. Human

Human Leaders are different. They are not necessarily driven or smart (but it helps).

What sets them apart is that they can somehow touch people on a human basis. Choose your own. Martin Luther King? JFK? John Lennon?

Let me tell you a story about such a Leader in my career. His name is Michael Baulk. Years ago, he was Managing Director of Ogilvy & Mather London. I was a young Graduate Trainee. In those days, Ogilvy recruited five grads a year. We weren't paid much, but we were very privileged.

A year into his career, one of my contemporaries approached Michael Baulk. He had fallen in love with a girl and wanted to take her on a romantic holiday to Africa – a holiday he knew he could not afford. He asked Michael Baulk if the company would advance him some salary to pay for this holiday. "Come back tomorrow", was the reply.

The next day, Michael Baulk got this young guy into his office and said: "I have checked with HR. I am sorry. They cannot do it. It would set a dangerous precedent. If they did it for you, they would have to do it for anyone else. I am sorry."

But guess what he did next? He got his cheque book out of his pocket and said: "But don't worry. I'll lend you the money myself. How much do you need? You have a successful career ahead of you. Have a great holiday. Pay me back when you can."

My friend (because, in those days, at Ogilvy, we were all friends) reminded me of this story 25 years later. He said he would always do anything for Michael Baulk. He has never forgotten him. And neither have I.

So there you go. Leadership with A Different Hat.

Be Driven. Be Smart. Be Human.

Better still, be all three.

Bet you can't.

4.2. THE QUEEN – NEVER COMPLAIN. NEVER EXPLAIN.

19 MARCH 2012 20:54

As you may know, this year, to honour Queen Elizabeth's Diamond Jubilee, the rest of the world has generously invited us to host the Olympic Games in London. On behalf of my Queen and I, I would like to thank you all.

Diamond Jubilee? If you did not know, that is sixty years on the throne. Or, as she may see it, sixty years of hard work. By any definition, that is a long career.

For the whole of this time, The Queen has lived by her mother's well-worn mantra: 'Never complain. Never explain.'

Online research attributes this maxim to such diverse figures as Benjamin Disraeli, Henry Ford, Frank Sinatra, Kate Moss and now, we are told, the mother of another Kate, Carole Middleton.

No matter. Let's stand back from this name-dropping and think about what The Queen, a world leader for longer than anyone else on this planet, has achieved as a human being. A person. A woman.

For sixty years, she has got up for work and out to face the world – quite literally face the world. Her whole life is on film. Her every move has been tracked and photographed. These days, no doubt, she has been warned of cameras pointing at her through every window of every house and every shrub in every garden.

In the face of all this attention, she has not said a wrong word and has not offended anyone (unlike her famously gaffe-prone husband). In fact, she does not appear to have said anything to anyone about anyone at all.

Starting, unbelievably, with Sir Winston Churchill, no one knows what she thinks of any one of the thirteen British, eleven Canadian, twelve Australian, fourteen New Zealand, nine Jamaican, seven Barbadian and three Bahamian Prime Ministers whom she has known – or, if I have

4.2. THE QUEEN – NEVER COMPLAIN. NEVER EXPLAIN.

counted right, the fifty-eight others from various other Commonwealth countries.

I am confident in saying that not one person on the planet has set eyes upon that many leaders, let alone worked with them. It is a lot of leaders. And a lot of tact. Because we do not know her opinion of any one of them.

If you use social media, you will have read a lot and you will have said a lot. The chances are, like me, you will have said more than you should – more, even than you may have wanted.

Yet, for sixty years, apart from formal speeches, The Queen has said nothing at all.

Is there a lesson in this? I think there is.

If you are in a position of leadership, perhaps you should say less than you do. You do not have to justify your every decision. You should not speak ill of anyone you work with. You need not criticise any of your customers or suppliers. You have no need to impress. Or preach.

Just get on with your job, set yourself the highest professional and personal standards, stand by them for the whole of your life and, while doing so, keep your mouth shut – and, certainly, never speak or write ill of any other person.

Then, like The Queen, and by example, you will win the admiration, loyalty and respect of everyone around you.

I am not saying this to curry favour or grovel.

I simply pay tribute to a remarkable woman.

And, in every sense, a life well led.

4.3. Richard Branson – Flexibility is the Key

13 March 2012 09:07

Thirty years ago, I first met Richard Branson, the founder of Virgin Records. His reputation was reclusive, perhaps even aloof. People knew about him, but they didn't know about him if you follow.

I had directions on how to find his houseboat moored on a canal behind some trees in North London. It was a cold, still day as the partly hidden old gate creaked open onto the towpath. I found the houseboat. I looked through the window. A pretty young lady was feeding a baby, holding it gently to her breast. Young as I was, I had never seen this before. She looked up, smiled and pointed to a rickety ladder and upwards.

Branson was sitting behind an equally rickety table, wearing a thick white jersey, with his arms crossed across his chest. He rocked slowly back and forth as he looked up and smiled. In front of him on the table was a large sheet of paper covered in scribbles and squiggles.

When I spoke, he looked at me with piercing eyes, still rocking back and forth. Sometimes he scribbled or doodled on the pad in front of him. There were moments of awkward silence. His responses were short but careful.

The meeting was about a magazine called Event which he had launched because the journalists at Time Out were on strike and he saw an opportunity. But – and this was why he wanted to see me – Time Out was now back in circulation and Event was not holding on to the once-orphaned Time Out readers.

Hidden behind these trees, on the towpath of this story are three lessons in leadership that have helped Branson in his success:

1. He kept himself out of the office. He was completely alone on the top deck of his family houseboat in the canal at Little Venice. Sure, Virgin Records was around the corner. But Branson wasn't. He kept a distance from the day-to-day.

4.3. RICHARD BRANSON – FLEXIBILITY IS THE KEY

2. He could spot an opportunity and move quickly to make it happen. With no top-heavy management structure and no massive overheads, he could take quick decisions and move faster than the competition.

3. He was prepared to move into new areas, moving with the market and the times. The sector has not mattered, just what he can bring to it. He is flexible.

This has been a defining characteristic of his career. Many of his products have failed including, as far as I know, Virgin Vodka, Virgin Cola, Virgin Vie, Virgin Bride and Virgin Others. Importantly, as with Event, he has known when to get out, as well as when to jump in. How many businesses are stuck in their business sector and model? Not Branson. He is flexible.

When he launched Virgin Atlantic, Branson could not compete with the promotional budgets of British Airways. For the sake of the business, the previously remote and socially uneasy Branson had to create his own PR stunts. Branson, himself, had to become the story. Even with his own persona, he was prepared to be flexible.

So where is he now?

With Virgin Atlantic financially strong enough to create its own marketing budgets (including a much-heralded 25th Birthday commercial with not a Branson in sight) Branson is more relaxed, more worldly in his perspectives.

With typical irreverence, he has written a book called 'Screw Business as Usual'. He has founded the not-for-profit Virgin Unite.

He says 'we must put the planet before profit'.

Having followed him since witnessing his lady feeding their baby thirty years ago, I reckon if Richard Branson is in this space then, surely, it is a good place to be.

4.4. WHEN YOU NEED SOMEONE TO DO SOMETHING THEY DON'T WANT TO DO

28 February 2013 09:03

Cynics might interpret the title of this post as a definition of marketing and, thus, the world we live in today. But, as marketing is my job, how could I agree?

One of the advantages of working in creative businesses is that, on the whole, decision-making is based on creative talent and strength of argument rather than rank or pay grade.

After all, you can't expect people to write what they don't think, draw what they can't see or film what they cannot imagine.

So, in the business sectors in which I have worked – music, publishing and advertising – people have the right to say no.

On the other hand, in the management of these businesses, there are times when you just have to persuade people to do things they might not want to do, however reluctant they might be, and for their own good as well as the business.

Once, I was managing the advertising for a large corporate conglomerate in whose portfolio was a relatively small French wine brand.

I knew the production budget would be unlikely to inspire any of the creative teams at my agency. But I did persuade the client that a visit to the vineyard in France might inspire better work than we might otherwise expect.

Our client, one of the best I have worked with, not only concurred but managed to borrow his company's private jet for what became a memorable and inspiring day – and advertising that was twice as effective as it might have been.

But I have never done anything, or had so much at stake as this:

Back in the day, Mike Oldfield was a jobbing musician hanging around the bars and clubs of London. He had sent early demos of Tubular Bells to every record company in town.

4.4. WHEN YOU NEED SOMEONE TO DO SOMETHING

No one was interested.

But Richard Branson, intent on launching Virgin Records, was captivated by the tapes and paid for the studio time Oldfield needed to record an album that would sell 18 million copies, spend over 300 weeks in the charts and earn royalties then, today and forever.

Furthermore, this one piece of work kicked off all of Branson's later success and was the launch-pad of the multi-billion pound Virgin empire that we know today.

However, back then, and just as Mike Oldfield had finished recording his masterwork, Richard Branson had a problem.

Recognising the need to promote this new product (he has been good at this in his career), Branson knew he needed to do something to launch it. As is often the case in creative industries, what better way to promote a product than the product itself?

Branson arranged a live recital at the Queen Elizabeth Hall.

Mike Oldfield was not keen on this idea. He was not keen at all. In fact he said no.

Tubular Bells had been meticulously constructed. Oldfield had played every instrument himself. A multitude of complex production issues had been overcome, including over 1,800 overdubs. Oldfield had not begun to consider the implications of performing his work on stage. The last thing he wanted to hear was 'Do it again but live!'

But, Richard Branson did not cancel the concert. He smoothed Mike Oldfield into his car – an old Bentley which his parents had bought for £300 and given him for his birthday.

On his way to the gig, and right at the last minute, Oldfield – again – told Branson he would not do it. He did not like it. He did not want it. He did not need it. He was exhausted. He had nothing left in the tank. It was all too much. There was no way he could play the concert.

Branson pulled over to the side of the road and the conversation went like this:

Richard Branson: 'If you can overcome your psychological problems and play this gig, the keys to the Bentley are yours.'

Silence for all of five seconds.

Mike Oldfield: 'I think I'm feeling slightly better!'

Oldfield gave a breathtaking performance and brought the house down.

And the rest is history.

Brilliant.

4.5. A MASTER CLASS IN THE ART OF CHAIRING A MEETING

16 December 2013 09:04

Lord Kingsdown died last month. He was best known as Chairman of the NatWest and then Governor of the Bank of England. I knew him as Robin Leigh-Pemberton and through playing cricket on the private ground at his estate in Kent.

They were happy days and a throwback in time.

Driving into the estate, and through a field to park in the long grass surrounding the ground; changing in the musty warmth of the 'pavilion' which, with no running water, was not much more than a shed; ambling slowly to the wicket to inspect the pitch; buffet lunch washed down with pints of freshly delivered Shepherd Neame (in the garage); and all in an air of genteel civility and the polite behaviour that Robin himself personified.

One day, we lined up to be introduced to Harold Macmillan as he sat in a deck chair to watch the cricket. Such was Macmillan's eyesight, I'm afraid, that I am sure he couldn't see who was shaking his gnarled, blotched, quivering hand let alone a cricket ball sixty yards away.

I don't meet many Prime Ministers so it was a special privilege for me to meet one who was at Oxford before the First World War where his friends were that select band of brothers who gave their lives for my freedom to play cricket in some corner of a field that is forever England.

From his obituaries, you might think Robin was a provocative figure. His appointment by Margaret Thatcher as Governor of the Bank of England was seen as the archest of old school tie arrangements. But he was 'far from being 'Thatcher's poodle' as critics of his appointment had feared – he proved determined to take his own line on European monetary union and Thatcher refused even to speak to him.'

4.5. A MASTER CLASS IN THE ART OF CHAIRING A MEETING

Me? As someone who despises the tribal loyalties of British politics based, as they are, on a bygone era, I have always preferred to judge people as I see them.

And I can say that Robin Leigh-Pemberton was as gentlemanly as an English country gentleman can be. He was kind, courteous and considerate. And generous. I happen to know he once congratulated a nineteen year old who had scored some runs by quietly slipping a fifty pound note into the teenager's hand: 'Well batted, young man. I hear you are off travelling. This might help.'

After more matches at Torry Hill, a letter arrived from his wife, Rose, asking me to raise a side for what was called Robin Leigh-Pemberton's XI against another team close to his heart. Thus, albeit a generation removed (I had played schoolboy cricket with two of their sons), I now came to know Robin and Rose on a more equal basis.

After his retirement from the Bank of England, and being that kind of guy, Robin became Chairman of the cricket club we played for and I realised he would be chairing our next committee meeting.

As I came to appreciate, attending his meetings was, truly, to witness a master at work.

I particularly admired the art of the quiet put-down, made possible by the knowledge that he was better prepared than anyone else around the table:

'Thank you Sam. That's a good point but I think you'll find we'll get to that under item five.'

'Thank you Nicholas. That's a very good point but we did discuss it at the last meeting, as I'm sure you have read in the minutes we have just approved.'

Or, sliding the glasses to the end of the nose, a quiet, cutting:

'Have you finished Jonny? Thank you. Shall we move on?'

Brilliant.

Early in my career at Ogilvy & Mather, we were trained how to manage meetings: make sure people are seated in the right place; that everyone has a copy of the agenda and, in those pre-tablet days, a pen and paper; and listen to, and take note of, what is being said.

Most important of all, do everything you can to think through and predict every eventuality in advance. Preparation is the key. Read the notes. Consider the facts.

Preparation, preparation, preparation.

And a tidy mind.

Yes, even in the creative businesses in which I have spent my career, there is no substitute for an ordered, uncluttered brain when it comes to managing a meeting.

By the way, one trick I was taught early in my career is how impressive it is, when speaking, to have the mental discipline to announce: 'There are five things I have to say' and then train your brain to remember all five with accuracy and in the right order.

I am sure you can learn these things.

Unforgivably, I digress. Let's return to the point at hand and why attending meetings chaired by Robin Leigh-Pemberton was, truly, to witness a master at work.

Surely the point of all meetings is to:

1. Consider the points on the agenda.
2. Listen to all points of view.
3. Reach a consensus.
4. Make decisions.
5. Agree next actions.

I can honestly say that in all the interminable meetings I have attended, it is very rare for at least one person not to repeat what they, or someone else, has said, speak off message, ramble on about insignificant trivia, make witless asides or crack unfunny jokes.

And, in so many of these meetings, my thoughts have strayed to the calm wisdom, the clear intelligence and, yes, the exceptional skill of Robin Leigh-Pemberton to work through an agenda in half the time anyone else could manage.

Attending his meetings was, truly, to witness a master at work.

All that remains is for me to convey my sympathies to the Leigh-Pemberton family and a Happy Christmas to all.

4.6. THE POPE'S OPPORTUNITY TO OVERCOME THE VESTED INTERESTS IN CHRISTIANITY

24 SEPTEMBER 2010 00:18

The Pope's visit to the UK at the end of last week and over the week-end dominated the media to such an extent that it is impossible to avoid the subject.

As a lapsed Catholic, who is now an atheist, I believe I have a right to my own say.

And I may have a world-changing Insight, in which the marketing and media industries could have a role. I am aware my Insights are not always accepted, not when I reveal them anyway, but I think I have one, which I will come to at the end.

For now, if it doesn't sound too biblical, please forgive me if I start at the beginning.

I experienced one of those strange British childhoods where, at the age of nine, I was sent to a Roman Catholic boarding school in Nottinghamshire. We had cricket pitches and football fields and woods to camp in. We had a swimming pool and bicycles to race around the grounds. Indoors, we had table-tennis and snooker tables.

But this was no English heaven – because my parents lived in Hong Kong.

So, in those days, 'home' was a 25-hour flight away including three sleep-denying stops such as Rome, Tel Aviv and New Delhi.

Leaving Hong Kong, at the end of the holidays, when it was time for us weeping, expatriate children to go back to school, BOAC employed extra people to tear us from our distraught parents and physically force us, kicking and screaming, onto the plane. One of the cabin crew held you down, the other fastened your seat-belt.

I don't think my parents liked this system but, in those days, it was 'the norm'.

Indeed, such was it the norm, that it was in my father's contract that the company, for whom he worked all his life, paid our school fees. At the end of the War, having served throughout the Middle East, he had ended up in India and, for a host of reasons, this lead to a successful career in the Far East, ending up in Hong Kong.

I have to admit that the little boy who the world now sees as privileged, because I was privately-educated, was profoundly miserable at school. For most of my adult life, I was able to compartmentalise this misery. I hid it away. Put it to one side.

Then, later, when my own kids reached the age of nine, all these negative thoughts came flooding back. Worse, I was jealous of my own kids coming home every day. That's quite heavy.

When I was their age, we attended Mass every morning. We 'served' at the altar. Confession was compulsory once a week, as were The Sacraments of the Cross.

So last week, the memories, the smells, the pictures in my mind and the inner misery of my Catholic prep school all came back. The Papal robes, the cassocks of his entourage, the hymns and the language were all scarily, creepily familiar. I could smell the incense on TV.

Because I feel entitled to a personal perspective, I come now to the various celebrities and 'opinion formers' who jumped on the Papal bandwagon.

Is Peter Tatchell really an opinion former? God forbid.

These people live in the 'secular' world which the Pope opposes. This was his key message. The USP of his trip.

Thanks to this issue, and its vast media exposure, the word 'secular' has attained new levels of awareness and infiltrated our lives – to the extent that 'secular' has defined itself as the antithesis of the word 'Pope'. Not Buddhism, not Islam, not even Protestantism.

Pope – secular. Secular – Pope. They go together. Except, of course, they don't.

The core issues which enrage our secular opinion formers are, it seems to me, fivefold – child abuse, contraception, abortion, homosexuality and women priests.

I have listed these five issues deliberately in the order above.

First, child abuse.

At my privileged Roman Catholic prep school, I was not abused. Well, I was, in that I was beaten almost weekly. The Headmaster had two leather

4.6. THE POPE'S OPPORTUNITY

slippers. One had a section of sole missing, which meant the nails stuck out so, for worse offences, you were patterned with six crescents of holes in your bum. These bled. The other slipper was full of sole (sic). This did not leave bloody marks but it bloody hurt.

I was not sexually abused. But I know it happened, by the Chaplain as it happens.

If them, why not me? Perhaps I was ugly. Hopefully, I was so unloved, miserable and stroppy that no one would touch me. Whichever way, lucky me.

My view on child abuse is that it is a criminal offence and that the law, however secular, overrides religious belief. So, if any Catholic priests, however senior, are found to have sexually abused children, then they should be prosecuted and punished. They can go to Hell, as far as I am concerned.

This includes anyone who may have covered up such behaviour. As I know from my own experience of litigation, covering up a criminal offence makes you an 'accessory to the crime'. Not that you necessarily get punished, of course. But you should be.

Anyway, last week, "Pope Benedict XVI admitted that the Catholic Church was too slow to tackle paedophilia by priests…(and)… apologised for the 'unspeakable crimes' committed by Catholic priests who sexually abused children". You can't say it clearer than that. However, as a lapsed Catholic, I can accept the apology but I am afraid you've still lost me.

Contraception. I do not agree with the Roman Catholic stance on this issue. In secular Britain, I believe this is an area of individual choice which most of us are capable of making. In other countries, without the benefit of wonderful health and educational systems such as ours, and where different values pertain, I think the Catholic position is positively dangerous and would argue against it. As a lapsed Catholic, this alone would keep me from the flock.

Abortion. This follows contraception or, rather, it doesn't. Ditto the above.

Homosexuality. Sorry, not my bag, but I don't agree. Live and let live.

Women priests. Of course there should be. No brainer.

So I am sorry Your Holiness, you have lost me. I am lapsed and staying lapsed.

But I have an Insight that might encourage me and many other atheists and non-Christians (not, note, non-Catholics but non-Christians) to change our atheist lives in our secular society.

Last week, you may even have taken the first couple of steps to executing the objective I am about to propose.

For the first time, you shook hands with a woman priest in Westminster Abbey.

For the first time, you visited the Archbishop of Canterbury in Lambeth Palace.

For the first time, you made an official Papal visit to Britain.

As supreme pontiff, pontifex maximus and vicar of Christ, you had a one-to-one chat with our Queen, defender of the faith and supreme governor of the Church of England.

So here's the deal.

Why don't you guys get together and unite all the Christian factions together to create one united Christian faith?

When I was young, I vowed I would never return to the Church until you all achieve this. If the leaders of the Catholic, Anglican, Baptist, Methodist, Lutherans and other Christian churches cannot join together, then why should I rejoin you?

I am very sad you cannot show this leadership. Frankly, if Northern Ireland can overcome their problems, why can't you guys get back together? You are the preachers.

Up and down this country, at our happiest and our saddest moments, when we are baptised or marry or mourn, we go to Church. But then, when we walk down your aisles and out of the doors of your historic churches and into your evocative graveyards to the sound of the most beautiful, resonant, moving music, you lose us.

I am the son of a Catholic mother and an Anglican father. My wife is Lutheran. We were married in a wonderful Cathedral in provincial Sweden.

And do you know what? Behind the main altar were three smaller Chapels and one of them was dedicated to Thomas à Becket. Like my family, he came from Kent.

Years later, one Christmas, as part of a school project, one of my children and I set out to discover why this English saint had been remembered in this way in the middle of Sweden. We discovered that

4.6. THE POPE'S OPPORTUNITY

Becket had fled to France and spent two years in the Cistercian abbey of Pontigny. There he made such an impression on some travelling Swedish priests that, when they heard of his later fate, they dedicated a Chapel in Linköping Cathedral to his memory. This was in the 12th Century, hundreds of years before Henry VIII wanted his divorce.

Now, in the 21st Century, wouldn't it be great if Christianity could unite and agree one set of values and transmit a modern, relevant social and moral message that would encourage us all back to Church to meet once more as local communities?

Wouldn't it be great if, rather than pontificating, you did this on a consensual basis? And wouldn't it be easy for you to get together and work out a way of communicating the Christian values you espouse? A message that, by defining the true Christian spirit and how we live our lives, we could all buy into and follow together as one Christian Church.

Then you could use your combined wealth to raise a budget to transmit this message using all the technological tools and human skills that we currently use to market cereal and washing powder to influence the behavioural values that unite rather than divide our society?

That, Your Holiness, would make your trip to Britain, and your cup of tea with the Queen, really worthwhile.

I believe, if he were to come back down to Earth, this is a brief Christ himself might set.

Until then, I fear that all the leaders of all the Christian churches are all too human to see the bigger picture and achieve this.

You have too many palaces, too much status, too much property, too much money, too much pride, too much baggage and too much to lose.

Ultimately, you have too many vested interests.

Pity.

4.7. What Sir Alex Ferguson could learn from David Ogilvy

25 April 2014 09:02

Who am I to add to the extraordinary volume of news articles about the sacking of David Moyes as manager of the Manchester United football team? On the Telegraph website alone there have been over 60 articles on this subject in the four days 22-24 April.

David Moyes' predecessor, Sir Alex Ferguson, is universally acknowledged to have been a master of his craft.

However, as someone who is not 'a football man', my abiding image of Sir Alex Ferguson is of him, after a game, gobbing a huge wad of chewing gum onto the revered Old Trafford turf before strutting into a post-match interview to complain about the ref. Couth? Not.

Having said this, it seems Sir Alex was hero worshipped by all the staff at Old Trafford where, we are told, he always had a kind word for the humblest of the staff: 'He possessed a compassionate side'. So who am I to judge?

In my observation, people who achieve great things do not always make brilliant decisions. Just like mere mortals, such as you and me, they can be stupid, unkind, boorish and pig-headed. And, because of this, they tend to polarise opinion. Think Mrs Thatcher.

Yet, having retired from a career in which he was undoubtedly successful, how brilliant has been the behaviour of Sir Alex since he retired?

1. He published a book in which he upset former players. Why did he do this? Surely not for the money.

2. He continued to watch his beloved Manchester United from the stands. Did he have to do this? Did it help David Moyes to have the club hero watching his every move?

4.7. WHAT SIR ALEX FERGUSON COULD LEARN FROM DAVID OGILVY

At my old school, there is a tradition that retiring headmasters do not set foot through the gates for seven years after they have left. Why couldn't Sir Alex have kept out of the way like this? Why not pour himself a glass of wine, relax in his favourite armchair and watch the game on TV? Isn't this what retirement is all about?

3. In many of the newspaper articles and online comments, it has been observed that it was Sir Alex who appointed (annointed?) Moyes as his successor.

How was this appointment conducted?

How professional was the process?

With what rigour were the candidates examined?

Whatever happened, it seems one crucial question may have been ignored:

'David, if you get this job, what will you do? How will you go about it?'

Surely, if he was asked this, Moyes would have had to declare that it was his intention to dismiss the incumbent senior management team and replace them with his own people?

In my own career, I saw this happen at Ogilvy & Mather.

David Ogilvy, the founder of O&M, urged senior managers to 'grow your own successor'. To encourage them to do this, with characteristic creativity, he sent each new company manager a Russian matryoshka doll – you know, the one you separate to reveal a smaller doll within, and then again, and then again.

With each doll came the message:

'If you hire people who are smaller than you are, we shall become a company of dwarfs. If you hire people who are bigger than you are, we shall become a company of giants.'

Sadly, when I was working for Ogilvy & Mather, an unusually talented Chairman and CEO team were prised away from us by a competitive agency. In a break with tradition, it emerged that their successors had not been grown from within O&M, but had been imported from another competitor.

In due course, the new, imported management team decided that it would be an idea to leave our iconic building overlooking the Thames to Canary Wharf. Unfortunately, the infrastructure at our new home had not been developed as promised and a whole generation of us, including me, left the company.

Last week, I returned to the Ogilvy office in Canary Wharf for the first time in 20 years and am delighted to say that it felt like the old Ogilvy culture seemed to be back in place – albeit, as far as I am concerned, in the wrong part of town.

David Ogilvy bequeathed numerous other words of wisdom which have helped to ensure the future success of a business he founded in New York in 1948.

Former employees of the agency continue to remind current employees of David Ogilvy's legacy:

'The house that Ogilvy built'

'What David Ogilvy meant to me'

'David Ogilvy and me'

All of these are well worth a read.

One cannot help but feel that if Sir Alex Ferguson, and other leaders, studied the David Ogilvy template they would enhance their reputations and leave the world a better place.

Remember: It's not what you achieve. It's the legacy you leave.

5
ADVERTISING

5.1. It may be right. It may be good. But is it interesting?

29 July 2014 19:26

David Ogilvy said this about advertising:

'You can't bore people into buying your product, you can only interest them into buying it.'

As my advertising career began with Ogilvy, I have been interested in 'interesting' for a very long time.

In today's world, is advertising interesting?

First, as any adman knows, we need to consider the competition which, in terms of interesting, includes all the other things that compete for people's interest.

Next, we need to establish whether there are different levels of interesting? Are all interestings equal? Or are some more interesting than others? How interesting does an interesting have to be to get noticed?

Is there a league table of interesting where, like those tedious research questionnaires, there is 'very interesting' at the top of the table and 'mildly interesting' at the bottom? Or is interesting more ruthless than this? It's interesting or it's not interesting. An interesting can be interesting but it can't be more interesting than another interesting. Is that how it is?

If you are not in, you are out.

Talking of cricket, to Englishmen like me the BBC Radio programme 'Test Match Special' (TMS) defines our Englishness by evoking happy memories of a balmy childhood, a poetic love of language, hazy cricket pitches on gentle village greens and the reassuring sound of willow caressing leather as the ball bumbles and bounds and bubbles to the boundary.

This week, England played India at Lord's, the home of cricket. Here, the imagery reflects a wider, more worldly hue. The Far Pavilions, the

Nawab of Pataudi, the flashing blade of Tendulkar, the hustle of Mumbai, the heat of Ganganagar and the chilly foothills of the Western Ghats. A world I have known only in words and pictures. But interesting? Yes, for sure.

This year, I have to confess, and hate to say it, and am aware of the treason of the offence, I have felt a feather of negative thoughts and creeping doubts while listening to TMS. I have begun to feel an increasing banality, a predictability, a repetitiveness I have not heard before.

How can this be?

Is it the prevailing media trend where retired cricketers, captains of their country no less, base their comments on the smug belief that if you did not spend years of your life playing cricket, interesting about cricket you cannot be? These people are beginning to bore me. Sorry.

Lesson One. If people find you interesting, don't take their interest for granted.

In my lifetime, another media institution has emerged. It is the TV arts programme, The South Bank Show. Earlier this summer there was a profile of John Lloyd, legendary producer of Not The Nine O'Clock News, Spitting Image and Blackadder.

I have discussed John Lloyd in another post. He said:

'Intelligence is something you're given. Kindness? That takes effort.'

Interesting thought, eh?

To me, John Lloyd is very interesting. What interests me most about him is his realisation that, as a BBC employee, he was not getting a share in the commercial success of the programmes he was instrumental in creating. He realised he would have to go it alone and create a 'format' which he owned and could develop and expand; and profit from himself.

And what interests me even more about John Lloyd is that not only did he recognise this need but he had the talent and intelligence and drive to do it.

He created QI.

QI stands for 'Quite Interesting'.

And so I find QI interesting but, as you would expect, only quite interesting. Perhaps this is why I rarely watch it. Don't get me wrong, if nothing else is on, if other people in the room are watching it, I am happy to watch QI. But I am only quite happy. For QI is not very interesting, is

5.1. IT MAY BE RIGHT. IT MAY BE GOOD.

it? It is only quite interesting. Actually, sometimes I find QI rather facile and even smug. And facile and smug are not very interesting either, are they? Not interesting at all.

Lesson Two. It is better to be very interesting than quite interesting.

Let's get back to advertising. Is advertising interesting? It should be. David Ogilvy said so.

Attracting my interest, these days, is very difficult. I have admitted my interest in Test Match Special and The South Bank Show. But, these days, I am bombarded with interesting like never before.

I have interesting meetings and interesting telephone calls. I receive interesting email and text messages. I find interesting articles on interesting websites. Interesting people say interesting things and link me to more interesting people and more interesting things on Twitter. My Facebook friends are interesting too. They link me to websites whose reason for being is interesting. I love the priest singing his sermon to Leonard Cohen's 'Hallelujah'. Interesting? Ok, perhaps not. But fun.

And get this. I never do anything without my iPad by my side. It is always with me. Whenever I am reading or watching or listening to anything interesting, I look up any number of thoughts that come to mind. How tall is that lady? Who did she marry? What films was she in? Isn't she dead? Questions such as this were interesting to me at the time but the next day, minutes later even, they become irrelevant and forgotten and no longer interesting at all.

Lesson Three. Do not assume that what you find interesting will interest other people.

There is a lot of interesting about.
Next year, there will be a General Election.
Will it be interesting?
Will the party leaders be interesting?
Will they have interesting things to say?
Will they have interesting new ideas to announce?
Will they develop more interesting ways of advertising themselves to us?
Will they have listened to the wise words of David Ogilvy?
It will be interesting to see, won't it?

5.2. STRATEGIC THINKING: SOME PEOPLE DON'T GET IT, DO THEY?

31 MAY 2013 09:04

Watching the BBC's The Apprentice, I am reminded of a show in last year's series when one of the contestants endlessly repeated 'What's the strategy? What's the strategy?' to a team leader who had no answer. Quite clearly, he didn't know what a strategy was (or is).

This meant that not only was the team very badly led but, as happens when no one knows what is going on, anarchy ensued.

Let's say the task was to make and sell a flavoured beer.
'What flavour should it be?'
'I like raspberry.'
'I like strawberry.'
'I like chocolate.'
'Ooh yes, I like chocolate too.'
'Let's make chocolate beer!'
'Great idea! Loads of people like chocolate.'
'So the colour will be chocolate brown?'
'That's boring. All beers are brown.'
'Lord Sugar won't like brown.'
'Yes he will. Brown Sugar!'
'My favourite colour is pink.'
'My favourite colour is yellow.'
'Mine's blue.'
'Ooh, yes! Blue's really in this year.'
'How about chocolate blue curaçao beer?'
'Great idea! I love curaçao.'
'Blue beer?
'Good point. Blue's not very chocolatey, is it?'

5.2. STRATEGIC THINKING: SOME PEOPLE DON'T GET IT, DO THEY?

'Or beery.'
'People love curaçao where I come from.'
'Where's that?'
'Lewisham.'
'I live in Edgware. Everyone drinks curaçao in Edgware.'
'Where shall we go then? Lewisham or Edgware?'
'Let's meet half way.'
'Great idea! Where's half way?'
'Whose got a map?'
'Look! Buckingham Palace is exactly half way between Lewisham and Edgware.'
'Lets go there!'
'Do you think the Queen likes blue beer?'
'She wore a blue dress last week.'
'And she's got blue blood!'
'I wonder how much beer she drinks?'
'She is the richest person in the country.'
'So she'll buy more than anyone else.'
'Cool. Let's go team!'
'Yeah!'
'Wow!'
'Sick!'
Doh.

You may not believe it, but I have attended 'creative' meetings like this in real life.

Funny, isn't it?

Surely it would not be beyond the wit of man to ask:

'What are we trying to achieve?'

and

'How are we going to do it?'

And bleeding well THINK!

5.3. STRATEGIC THINKING: BE DECISIVE BUT KEEP AN OPEN MIND

14 JUNE 2013 09:04

In life, there are only three decisions you need to get right – and one of them is where you live.

In a TV programme called Escape to the Country, couples are helped to move house from an urban to rural location. The format of the programme is simple:

- introduction to the location
- review of local house prices
- meet the 'movers'
- see House One
- see House Two
- see House Three (the 'mystery house')
- discussion of preferred options

This is the 'format' and, in the TV world, there is crucial meaning behind that word.

Successful formats make production companies rich. Indeed, such are the fortunes made that 'formats' are precisely defined – and fiercely defended.

Escape to the Country contains two features which are crucial to its format.

One is that, after they have seen a house, our movers have a little competition between them to guess its market price. This is rather a meaningless task, as the presenter could just tell them, but it is essential to the format – a usp if you like. Pointless (sic) but valuable.

The 'mystery house' is also key. This is where our couple, having defined the sort of home they would like to move to, are shown a house that the programme makers know is outside the brief that has been provided.

5.3. STRATEGIC THINKING: BE DECISIVE BUT KEEP AN OPEN MIND

In Escape to the Country, the presenter makes a huge issue of the mystery house. It helps the production company, in that dreadful phrase, make the format their own.

And it never ceases to surprise me how often our couple fall in love with the mystery house rather than the other options which more closely match their brief.

It is surprising because, as this is going to be their home, you would have thought they could work out what they want.

But no, in the mystery house, an outside perspective has helped them realise their own dreams.

What can we learn from this?

A strategy is the simple definition, and careful analysis, of what one wants to achieve and how one is going to do it.

Yet, as this rather simple TV format shows, however hard one thinks through one's strategy – and, perhaps, the closer one is to it – the greater the benefit of an objective perspective.

This is why, usually, external agencies are more successful than in-house teams.

For, however much you have researched your strategy, and however hard it has been to define what you want to achieve and how you are going to do it, it remains vital to listen to the views of others.

As evidenced by Escape to the Country, you can become so close to an issue that you can't see the wood from the trees.

5.4. How the UK Government ignored the most basic law of advertising

11 October 2013 09:07

The Rt Hon Theresa May, Secretary of State for the Home Office has announced that she wishes to create a 'hostile environment' for illegal migrants to Britain. But early attempts to do this run the risk of alienating those of us who have every right to be here.

In July, the Home Office, led by Ms May, launched an advertising campaign against illegal immigrants to the UK. The chosen message was as follows:

> IN THE UK ILLEGALLY?
> 106 ARRESTS LAST WEEK IN YOUR AREA
> GO HOME OR FACE ARREST
> TEXT HOME TO 78070 FOR FREE ADVICE.

The media channel used to transmit this message was 'poster vans' which were driven through six London boroughs where, apparently, 'illegal immigrants are likely to be'.

I was one of many who found this to be a particularly tasteless piece of work and posted to this effect on Twitter and LinkedIn. But 224 people felt more strongly than me and complained to the Advertising Standards Authority (ASA) who, this week, ruled:

'The ad must not appear again in its current form. We told the Home Office to ensure that, in future, they held adequate substantiation for their advertising claims and that qualifications were presented clearly.'

In relation to the phrase 'GO HOME', the ASA weasled as follows:

'We acknowledged that the phrase "GO HOME" was reminiscent of slogans used in the past to attack immigrants to the UK... We recognised that the poster, and

5.4. HOW THE UK GOVERNMENT IGNORED THE MOST BASIC LAW

the phrase "GO HOME" in particular, were likely to be distasteful to some in the context of an ad addressed to illegal immigrants… However, we concluded that the poster was unlikely to cause serious or widespread offence or distress.'

Whatever the ASA have found, who are the people who thought up and created this distasteful piece of work – and who on earth approved it?

Whoever they are, surely they must know that all advertising in the UK must be:

Legal, decent, honest and truthful

The ASA makes no secret of this requirement:

'Our mission is to ensure that advertising in all media is legal, decent, honest and truthful, to the benefit of consumers, business and society.'

'Legal, decent, honest and truthful' is a phrase that was cemented into my mind on the first day of my advertising career. It is the DNA of the UK advertising business.

I will leave it to you to judge whether these posters were 'decent' or 'to the benefit of society' or not, but there is an even more fundamental aspect of advertising of which the Home Office seems to have been ignorant; or ignored.

As ever, David Ogilvy said it for me:

'Do not address your readers as though they are gathered together in a stadium. When people read your copy, they are alone.'

This is the most basic law of advertising and one that I have stuck to throughout my career. It is, if you like, in my own professional DNA.

It means that, however you define your 'target audience' in terms of the media you select, the content of your message must be such that you would be comfortable to say it to one person – not some amorphous group.

Whether you are in advertising or marketing or the media or are ever anything to do with the communications business, you must remember that any form of communication between human beings is a one-to-one thing.

I cannot over-emphasise how important this is.

So let's re-look at this poster van and consider its 'GO HOME' message as a transmission from the Home Office to one person – alone.

For example, what would happen if Theresa May were to stand outside an underground station in London and – for this is what this poster did –

say to passers by on a one-to-one basis in this multi-racial, multi-cultural, cosmopolitan capital city of ours?

'Are you in the UK illegally? GO HOME.'

'Are you in the UK illegally? GO HOME.'

'Are you in the UK illegally? GO HOME.'

It might be that such an approach would not only provoke the 'hostile environment' Theresa May seeks but also a hostile response.

For, if she carried on behaving like this and continued to transmit her slogan to each passer by, she might be arrested by the police for breaching the peace or causing an affray – or even, perhaps, a riot.

And then, subject to the extent of the affray and damage caused, she might even find herself sentenced to a spell in prison.

And which Government Department is responsible for police and prison?

Yes, you've guessed it. The Home Office.

You couldn't make it up, could you?

5.5. MAN'S INHUMANITY TO MAN

18 MARCH 2010 12:36

A seminal moment in my life came when I was one of the first European business managers to visit Vietnam.

At the time, I was the General Manager of Ogilvy & Mather in Thailand. Our US clients were embargoed from engaging with Vietnam and our European and Thai clients wanted to find potential business opportunities in the Vietnamese population of 70 million 'consumers' before their American competitors were allowed in.

I was told I would have a 'guide' but that, really, he was a Government employee who would report back on all of my movements. A spy.

At the War Museum in Saigon, in rows of glass jars, were the deformed embryos which had been conceived by Vietnamese mothers whose homes had been blanket-bombed by napalm, dropped by American airplanes.

During this trip, I was constantly urging my guide that I was European, not American.

He told me I did not need to do this. The Vietnamese held nothing against Americans.

After all "we won the war" he claimed "but what we couldn't understand was that the Americans were bombing us in South Vietnam when our leaders told us they were on our side".

Of course, the Americans could not tell the difference between a North Vietnamese enemy citizen from a South Vietnamese friendly citizen – so they decided to bomb the lot of them.

And, I fear this rather ruthless military strategy may have caused the appalling, and unforgivable, suffering to the children of Fallajuh in Iraq.

We are told that we are in Iraq and Afghanistan to win over the 'hearts and minds of the people'.

Yet when President Obama, who inherited this mess, wanted to win over the hearts and minds of Republican voters to win the US election, did he do it by sending in the troops, by shooting people or by dropping bombs?

Of course he didn't. He used sophisticated 'new media' techniques.

Do we, here in cosy Britain, with a General Election looming, know who votes Conservative and who votes Labour? No, of course we don't.

And I don't think even our ruthless and unprincipled politicians will be blanket-bombing us all in the hope that they will mop up the other side.

And now consider what happened when it emerged that thousands of Iranians felt that their election in Iran had been fixed. What did they do?

They used new media channels, especially Twitter, to protest at what was happening. In June 2009, the BBC reported: 'Although there are signs that the Iranian government is trying to cut some communications with the outside world, citizen journalism appears to be thriving on the web.'

Yet, when it comes to us communicating to them, we send in the tanks.

Where is the media strategy that we could develop, and media intelligence we could apply, to work alongside our brave Army soldiers?

In Iraq or Afghanistan, how on earth can these brave servicemen and women tell the Al Qaeda or the Taliban from the rest of the population?

Recently, I heard a radio report that an issue facing our brave servicemen and women in Afghanistan is that The Taliban disguise themselves as local people, enter a village, lay a few bombs, blow up some soldiers and then disappear back into the hills.

What if we provided the villagers (who presumably know who all the Taliban insurgents are but are too scared to say) with the media technology such as laptops and mobile phones to keep our soldiers, or select 'middle men', informed as to the presence of our real enemies within?

And how differently would our Army be perceived if, instead of firing guns and parading around in tanks and dropping bombs as well, of course, as dying for the cause themselves, they handed out laptops and mobile phones and urged the people to listen to the reasons why we are there?

Wouldn't it help these poor people, in these poor countries, if we told them more clearly and more often what we are doing there and what we are fighting for – human rights, the difference between right and wrong, the rule of law, the importance of education, respect for others, 'do as you would be done by', tolerance, freedom of speech, liberty, democracy?

Quite apart from the lives lost, the BBC have reported that the ultimate size of the bill for the wars in Iraq and Afghanistan could reach

5.5. MAN'S INHUMANITY TO MAN

$3 trillion ($3,000bn). That is a lot of second-hand laptops and mobile phones.

So, my proposal is to allocate just a small percentage of these vast costs to develop a media strategy to communicate what we are up to.

If millions of Americans and Europeans cannot understand why we are in Iraq and Afghanistan, how on earth can we expect the indigenous people to have a clue what we are doing there either?

I believe passionately that, as one of the great 'creative' countries of the world, we should be developing a more sophisticated approach. We have the expertise to persuade people to change the way they behave. It is called Behavioural Economics.

But I do not believe we use our skills in this area to help overcome the really important things in our society or in the wider world.

Instead, we have our creative, media and communications experts using meerkats to sell insurance and a gorilla to sell chocolate.

Come on, we can do better than this.

(Please see my book 'Ideas for Britain' for further discussion of various social issues).

6
MARKETING

6.1. Marketing = Consumers = Customers = Cash

31 July 2013 09:04

And so, as we enjoy our short, hot summer, a new generation of university graduates return their rented gowns and mortar boards and head off into the big, wide world.

The lucky ones know what they want to do and are taking the first steps to fulfilling their dream of becoming a doctor or a lawyer or, God forbid, a banker.

Some will seek to monetise their talent in the arts by maximising the life-changing royalties their talent can bring. Others will have sporting ambitions and dreams of glory, perhaps, in the Olympics in Rio, in 2016.

Some won't have a clue what they want to do.

And some, young as they are, will have a business idea that will change the world.

At about the same age, when I was 23, I had such a dream.

My thought was to capitalise on the explosion of a new-fangled boom called the audio cassette – and a thing called the Walkman that enabled you to listen to music on the move.

This led to the iconic SFX – the world's first music magazine on audio cassette.

While it is true that, as a business, SFX lasted less than two years, I feel entitled to remind you that our first issue sold an audited 58,000 copies in London alone.

This meant that, once the 'content' had been created, it had been copied (in a day) onto 58,000 cassette tapes which were distributed, in bulk, to thousands of newsagents for 58,000 customers, who had been made aware of this brand new concept through old media, to part with 50p each to buy them.

Nowadays, of course, in the digital world we live in, there are much easier 'routes to market' than this.

You don't need the capital to build a factory or a production line.

You don't need lorries to distribute your product (deliver, perhaps – 'distribute', no).

You don't need to pay rent for a shop on the high street (or be bullied by the major multiples).

You don't even need to pay for the media space to communicate the brilliance of your idea to potential customers.

But there is one thing that will never change – and that one thing, let me tell you, is the meaning of the word 'customers'.

Customers are people who pay you money for whatever it is you have produced to sell them.

Customers are not 'followers' or 'friends'.

Customers are not 'likes' or 'shares'.

Customers are not 'clicks'.

Customers = cash.

Never forget this.

A 'consumer' only becomes a 'customer' once you've been paid.

I cannot tell you the number of great new business ideas that pass my way where the enthusiastic management team have failed to fully understand consumer response to their sexy new idea and, within this failing, another axiomatic mathematical formula:

Consumers = customers = cash.

You may think this naïve. If so, you would be surprised to know how naïve otherwise intelligent and sophisticated business people, including bankers, can be.

I cannot tell you how many business plans, and financial forecasts, have passed my way which include an expenditure line called 'marketing' without a clue what this means.

For when you ask these sophisticated financiers who the marketing expenditure will be aimed at, what it is aimed to achieve, how it will achieve it and how much cash it will generate, they look at you with eyes as blank as an empty column in a spreadsheet.

Usually, they argue that 'marketing' is a fixed percentage of 'revenue'. They fail to understand that revenue is a function of marketing – not the other way round.

6.1. MARKETING = CONSUMERS = CUSTOMERS = CASH

And, as numbers people, all they get back from me, a people person, is yet another axiomatic financial formula:

Marketing = consumers = customers = cash.

I accept that some of the world's most highly valued new media businesses have attracted extraordinarily large customer bases and then tried to work out how to monetise them – but did Facebook or Twitter have 58,000 paying customers in the week they launched? Did they?

I would argue that these are the exceptions that prove the rule so, whether you are a student or a high-flying banker, I have provided you with the 1-2-3 of marketing:

1. Customers = cash.
2. Consumers = customers = cash.
3. Marketing = consumers = customers = cash.

Forget this at your peril.

Or it will cost you.

6.2. BRANDING: UNDERSTANDING THE IMPORTANCE OF TRUST

23 APRIL 2013 09:04

When I joined the advertising business, there was a new buzzword called 'marketing'. Few knew what it meant. At Ogilvy & Mather, where my career was born, we had a guy – yes, one person in the whole agency – whose job was to explain this new concept to our clients.

Now, some people argue, everything is marketing.

In his wonderful, intelligent lecture on screenwriting, Charlie Kaufman said:

'They're selling you something. And the world is built on this now. Politics and government are built on this. Corporations are built on this. Interpersonal relationships are built on this… it has all become marketing.'

In this sense, within the space of my career, marketing has gone from nothing to everything.

That's some journey.

Now, it seems, there is another word that is commonly used and little understood. It is the word brand, the application of which is called 'branding'.

What is branding?

There is no easy answer for, as David Ogilvy said,

'Brand image is an amalgam of many things – name, packaging, price, style of advertising, and, above all, the nature of the product itself.'

'The nature of a product' can be defined in terms of 'rational' and 'emotional' benefits.

If your clients tell you the truth, rational benefits are easy to identify. The trouble is the rational benefits of a product are often the same as its competitors. Commercial success depends on the identification, and often creation, of emotional points of difference.

6.2. BRANDING: UNDERSTANDING THE IMPORTANCE OF TRUST

I love this part of my job because, to define the emotional values of a brand, you need to understand how human beings think and behave.

And, as I hope you find in all my posts, people are interesting, aren't they?

This is why the best way to understand a brand is to think of it as a person, a human being, replete with a complex blend of rational and emotional characteristics.

In life, the way we behave influences other people to like or dislike us on a sliding scale. If you are nice, people like you. If you are horrid, they don't. You may or may not care about this.

But brands do care whether or not you like them, particularly if they want you to buy them.

So what is the one thing brands must do to make you like them? Again, David Ogilvy has the answer. He called it a consumer promise:

'A promise … is a benefit for the consumer. It pays to promise a benefit which is unique and competitive, and the product must deliver the benefit you promise.'

To deliver a promise, a brand must tell the truth.

And people must trust the brand to do so.

Sadly, it seems, trust is an evaporating characteristic in society today. For example, although you and I trust our doctors, politicians don't ('Can your doctor be trusted, or not?').

Who, in my life, have I trusted in the past but trust no more?

I won't name individual brands, but here are some of the sectors they are in:

I don't trust cyclists.
I don't trust horse racing.
I don't trust food companies.
I don't trust supermarkets.
I don't trust loyalty cards.
I don't trust marketing.
I don't trust newspapers.
I don't trust banks.
I don't trust business.
I don't trust priests.
I don't trust the police.
I don't trust politicians.
You?

6.3. The difference between a commodity and a brand

14 November 2013 09:04

An abiding memory of my career is sitting on a pavement in Saigon pouring hundreds of cans of lager down the drain.

As an expert in the potential of the Vietnam market, having been there once before, I was with a regional director of Heineken. He carried a widget on his keyring by which he could identify the origins of every single can of his beer, including full details of when and where it had been brewed.

Yet, even if the beer was only marginally out-of-date, we bought it from the shops at full price and into the gutter it went.

As imported beer was illegal in Vietnam at the time, I asked the Heineken man why he felt it was so important to do this. Surely this stock had been smuggled in illegally? It cannot have been sourced from official Heineken distributors, can it? Why was he responsible?

He said it was very important that, wherever and whenever it was sold, Heineken had to be in absolutely perfect condition. Any beer which did not meet Heineken's rigorous quality standards must be disposed of. The integrity of the brand was – and presumably still is – paramount.

And so we sat, for well over an hour, pulling rings and pouring Heineken down the drain.

As I have posted before, the marketing of brands is based on a consumer promise. There is an unwritten contract between you and the manufacturer that you will get what you pay for.

My life can be defined by relationships like this: Johnson's Baby Shampoo, Weetabix, Marmite, Heinz Baked Beans, Guinness, Laphroaig …

It must be difficult for the manufacturers of these brands to ensure such a consistently high level of product quality. But they do. They work very hard to deliver the consumer promise they have made. So, as I trust them to do this, I keep buying their product. They have my 'brand loyalty'.

6.3. THE DIFFERENCE BETWEEN A COMMODITY AND A BRAND

Furthermore, as these brands offer me something unique – something special, something I cannot get from anywhere else – their personalities and mine become welded together.

I like having these brands in my life. We have an emotional connection.

There are other products for whose suppliers I feel no such affiliation, no loyalty, no emotional connection at all. In fact, along with many of their customers, I dislike them intensely.

The most topical of these are household energy 'products'.

When it comes to gas and electricity there are no product differentiators, no unique benefits, no 'taste' promises to fulfil.

Gas is gas.

Electricity is electricity.

The companies that compete to sell me these 'products' are middle men. Commodity brokers.

And, as I feel no affinity with their commodity products, I have no 'loyalty' to them at all. Buying them is a purely rational decision. They give me no emotional reward whatsoever.

Household energy is what marketing people call a distress purchase.

I don't want to buy gas and electricity, I have to – otherwise my family will freeze or starve. And what makes it worse is that every household in the UK has to buy them too.

The energy suppliers know this.

They also know that, just as I want to buy their commodity products as cheaply as possible, so it is their job to extract as much money from as many people as they can.

To achieve this, as they have no product differentiators and no brand integrity (unlike Heineken), all they can do is dream up ever more complex, fanciful financial bundles to secure 'customer loyalty'.

The more complex the bundles, the more confusing they become. The more confused they are, the more likely it is that customers will pay more than they need to. And you're never going to trust anyone who has conned you into paying more than you need, are you?

So it is that, in commodity markets, the only loyalty suppliers can attract from their customers is to 'lock' them into long-term fixed contract for periods of, say, five years. This is not 'customer loyalty'. It is 'customer entrapment'. That's what being 'locked in' means, isn't it? Imprisonment.

If you are imprisoned, you are not free.

And so – as I hope I have shown in this and my previous post – in today's day and age, where we are supposed to be living in a sophisticated free market economy, household energy is a ridiculously manufactured market which is not 'free' at all?

It is a concoction.

Or, as some might have it, a con.

And that's the problem, isn't it?

6.4. The difference between a product and a service

29 November 2013 09:06

In my last post, I shared my experience of pouring hundreds of cans of beer down the drain in Vietnam due to the high level of care Heineken take to ensure that every can of their lager meets their strict quality standards.

I mentioned several more of my favourite brands that, presumably, are managed in the same way: Johnson's Baby Shampoo, Weetabix, Marmite, Heinz Baked Beans, Guinness, Laphroaig.

I am sure you have your favourites too.

Brands like this are known in the trade as Fast Moving Consumer Goods (FMCG) – and the CV of anyone who is anyone in marketing is strengthened by FMCG experience.

The easiest way to understand FMCG products is to think of them as products sold in the 'major multiples' (supermarkets to the great unwashed): fresh food, chilled food, frozen food, fruit and veg, milk and dairy, toiletries, household cleaning etc. These products, which we use and consume on a daily basis, are the staple diet of the supermarket business.

Yes, I know that, in their bigger stores, the supermarkets have expanded into white goods, brown goods, books and clothing, none of which are FMCG products.

I know the range of products offered by the supermarkets online is vastly greater than the stock on the shelves in their shops.

And I know that you can buy these products in other retail outlets such as corner shops, which are known in the trade as 'CTNs' (Confectioners, Tobacconists and Newsagents).

There is no love lost between CTNs and supermarkets.

And, as I have written in my next post, I have a particular admiration for the couple who manage my local corner shop.

But I also listened to the thoughtful defence of his sector by Sir Terry Leahy, the former CEO of Tesco, on Desert Island Discs. One-sided, perhaps, but also human:

'If you talk to people, you will find that 95% of the population like supermarkets. 5% don't. But of course, in Britain, 5% is 3 million people. They have a voice and right to say what they think… You have to be careful to make sure that you are creating things which are beneficial. You are not manipulating the customer. The best organisations do put their customers at their heart.'

Sir Terry was also interesting on how his modest background helped him relate to the people in his company which he felt was his most important responsibility in his job.

We don't often think of the people who work in supermarkets, do we?

I visit a regular round of supermarkets: Waitrose, Co-op, Tesco every week; Sainsbury and M&S every so often – and I can say that I enjoy relating to all of the people who work in these places. They are invariably polite, friendly and helpful and a credit to their companies.

While it is a challenge for supermarkets to keep their shelves stocked with fresh, up-to-date products all spick-and-span with their fancy packaging, they also manage the bit between the customer selecting a product from the shelves and walking out of the door particularly well.

This part of the process is called service.

And, even in the highly automated world of major multiple retailing, the human aspect of their business – customer service – is very important.

Yet, some businesses have nothing to offer other than the service they provide.

These companies, unlike those in the FMCG sector, don't have ingredients to buy, factories to manufacture their products, or sales forces to sell them, marketing companies to brand them, supermarkets to negotiate with, or distribution networks to transport them around the country.

Services are all they have.

You know the companies I am talking about – mobile phones, insurance, water, gas, electricity etc. They don't have to work very hard or do very much, do they? As I hope I showed last time, all they are is middle men. Brokers.

6.4. THE DIFFERENCE BETWEEN A PRODUCT AND A SERVICE

How did you feel when you last engaged with O_2 or Vodafone or Direct Line or eSure or Thames Water or Severn Trent or British Gas or EDF or nPower?

Not a very appealing bunch, are they?

But these people depend on the point of human interaction as their most crucial point of the purchasing process. This is the moment when the customer presses the 'buy' button online or reads out their credit card details on the phone.

What emotional reward have any of these companies ever given you?

They certainly don't fill you with the warmth of human kindness that I feel at the check-out counters in my local supermarkets.

Yet, as it is all they have, you would think the human interaction when we engage with these businesses would be at the very top end of the emotional spectrum.

But they are not are they?

We still have to press a number on the phone to choose the right option, listen to excruciating muzak while we hang on the line and understand the local accent of wherever in the world their call centre is based.

Online, we don't get an emotional reward from buying things either. With all the technology in the world, can't these people find a way of showing me they care? All it would take is a pop-up of a human being to smile at you and say thank you.

And what about our public services? Have they got 'their customers' at their heart?

Do you know anyone who has fallen on hard times and needs to sign on the dole?

Or do you know anyone who has got sick and needs to claim disability benefit?

Do you?

Have you any idea of the indignity of the process, where the assumption they are on the take overrides the care they need?

I have described my own experience of this inhuman process in my book *'Ideas for Britain'* ('Disability Living Allowance (DLA) Disgrace').

Public service?

Humanity?

Care?

You must be joking.

97

I do think it is very important for us to remember, at all times, that as soon as we use the word 'service', the word 'human' should be attached inextricably to it.

What a sorry state we are in when our public services can't match the personality of a pack of Corn Flakes.

6.5. THE HUMAN IMPORTANCE OF CUSTOMER SERVICE (1)

20 October 2010 07:07

Earlier this year, my family and I moved home. We didn't move far. Just one side of Clapham Common to the other (and still in Battersea, of course).

At our old house, where we had lived for nearly 20 years, I had become used to the habit of reading the newspaper over a brew and toast before heading off for work. This was a small piece of English life that I had sorely missed in the overseas posting that my agency had told me would advance my advertising career.

After our move (in Battersea, not from the other side of the world) I found, to my horror, that the nearest newsagent didn't do home deliveries. He told me: "It's too much trouble managing the delivery persons" (that's PC-speak for paper boys).

Well, back at our previous house, if the paper wasn't delivered early in the morning, my whole routine broke down. The time taken to walk the short distance to the newsagent and back would start my day on completely the wrong footing.

Before you accuse me of laziness, I made a rule to myself that I would walk to the shop and buy my own newspapers on Saturdays and Sundays. This also allowed me a cheery face-to-face greeting and some friendly banter with the newsagent and/or his wife.

This couple are called Sachin and Shilpa (well they are not actually – their names have been changed to protect their privacy).

As human beings, I admire Sachin and Shilpa as much as anyone I have met.

For the whole time I have known them, which is since 1991, they have missed only one day serving their customers in their shop. This was for a family funeral.

And when I say 'one day' I mean ONE DAY, including Saturdays and Sundays, in nearly 20 years.

And when I say one 'day', I mean a DAY that starts at 5am and ends at 8pm.

A long day. Day after day. Year after year.

Sometimes, my newspaper of choice would be late from the wholesaler. On these occasions, I would receive an alternative newspaper with a little note of apology explaining the situation and saying that I could, of course, swap the paper for my preferred option later in the day. They would put it to one side just in case.

On other occasions, when I bought a Birthday Card, they would ask who the card was for and, if it was for one of our children, they would give them a chocolate bar or whatever they knew was their favourite confection.

When we went on holiday, in post- as well as pre-internet days, they knew I hated missing out certain pieces of news (including, as it happens, the Business pages). For however long the time away, they would keep my newspaper in a pile in their already jam-packed shop. And when I returned, there they would be, all neatly sorted by day – beginning with the first date first, at the top of the pile.

So now we have moved house, I have to walk to the closest newsagent and buy my newspaper from there. Or, as my small moment of morning pleasure is denied me, I pick it up somewhere else later in the day. Sadly mid-week, Sachin and Shilpa's shop has become just too far a walk.

But, at week-ends, what do I do?

I drive past a number of other newsagents to buy my paper from Sachin and Shilpa's shop, as I have for nearly 20 years. They say 'Good Morning' and 'How Are You?' and 'Thank You' and, if they are not busy serving their other customers, we have a little chat.

I treasure their friendship.

My friendship with, and certainly my admiration for, this wonderful couple stems from the fact that day-in, day-out, for better or for worse, in sickness and in health, they have looked after their customers like me.

You may have noticed the word 'Ryanair' in the headline of this post but that, until now, I have not used this word at all.

And I am not going to use it again. Once is quite enough.

If you have been a customer of this airline, you will know why.

If you have not been a customer of this airline, look after yourself.

6.6. THE HUMAN IMPORTANCE OF CUSTOMER SERVICE (2)

29 OCTOBER 2014 09:30

The man dozed.

For the first time in over a year, he could lie-in late in bed. Time to rest from the hassles of home. Phew. Two weeks alone on the Greek Island he loved and … 11

Bang! Bang! 'Cleaning!'

Bang! Bang! 'Cleaning!'

The man hauled himself out of bed and his day dreams. He grabbed his favourite kikoy from the bottom of the bed, wrapped it around the middle of his body and opened the door of his perfectly comfortable hotel room.

'Cleaning!'

'Now? Really? I'm tired'.

'Cleaning!'

'I only got here last night. The room's fine.'

'No speak English! Cleaning!'

One was dark haired, the other an unlikely blonde. There were no uniforms. Not here. Not in this small, lovely, informal family hotel with stunning sea views. Just two poor ladies in cheap jeans and T-shirts. Getting by. Doing a job. Unsmiling. Unmoving.

'Ok, ok. Two minutes.'

'Cleaning!'

Unsmiling. Unmoving.

The man raised his hand in a sign to wait and shut the door. Hurriedly, he daubed a toothbrush round his mouth and pulled on his swimming trunks. He threw sun cream, baseball cap, shades and a beach towel into a kit bag and, from the unpacked suitcase, grabbed the vital, still boxed lilo.

'Yassu.'

The man forced a smile as he moved out of the room.

'Yassu.'

Unsmiling, the ladies moved in.

Walking out of the building and into the sun, the man captured the perfect view of the bay as he crossed the patio to the spacious pool. He chose a sun bed and reached for the lilo. Blow, blow, blow. The familiar holiday ritual. One blow. And another. And another.

He put on the cap and the shades and grabbed the book. He dropped the towel by the pool and the lilo into it. Halfway down the steps into the cool, clean water, he turned, reached down under his legs and found the lilo with his left hand. He lowered himself onto it and launched himself backwards into the pool. The book in his right hand stayed dry. He still had it.

For over an hour he read, dozed and read on the lilo. He dreamt of what the future might hold and ...

'Yak, yak! Jabber, jabber!'

'Yak, yak! Jabber, jabber!'

The cleaning ladies were seated at a table in the restaurant by the pool. Presumably, their morning break. They smoked roll-up cigarettes and spoke loudly. Very loudly. Not Greek, but an unknown Eastern European language. They were not smiling. They were arguing. Loudly.

Around the pool, the hotel guests raised their eyebrows at each other, shook their heads and put down their books. Some questioned whether they would return to this hotel.

Fifteen minutes later, the hotel workers left their table and normal service was resumed.

And then it was time for lunch. The man found a table shaded by a large umbrella in the corner of the patio, by a wall. He ordered a Mythos beer and a Greek salad. Just what he wanted.

Looking out towards the azure sea and the clear blue sky, he swigged his beer, leant back and ...

He smelt a cigarette. Behind him, the blonde cleaner, also taking advantage of the shade, was sitting on the wall, not six feet away. She looked up as her friend joined her with two glasses of cola. Unsmiling, she took the cigarette from her mouth, handed it over and started rolling another. They resumed the argument. Loudly.

The man wanted to help these poor ladies.

But how could he?

6.7. Books : 'Form is temporary. Class is permanent.'

24 January 2012 21:36

'Form is temporary. Class is permanent.' This saying, heard most often in my life in a cricketing context, came to mind today as I was helping to judge the BMS Seasonal Book Marketing Awards (a much more modest event than today's Costa Book Awards, won by Andrew Miller's novel *'Pure'*).

One BMS entrant was the campaign celebrating the centenary of the birth of William Golding and, inevitably, his seminal novel 'Lord of the Flies'. I know not everyone likes the book but that black-and-white film and its mantra 'Kill the Pig, Kill the Pig' haunted me throughout my lonely, scary boarding school childhood.

The marketing idea was to invite children to design a new cover for the book. But the real delight was the opportunity to look back at the beautifully designed and wonderfully crafted covers that have graced 'Lord of the Flies' since it was published in 1954.

There can be no greater conjugation of literature and art than these.

The same observation can be applied to Gary Oldman's performance, and today's Oscar nomination, in the recent film of the book 'Tinker Tailor Soldier Spy'. Of course, the book was reprinted alongside the film. But why not push Le Carré's entire canon? What an opportunity to connect another class act to a whole new generation of readers!

In this digital age, 'class is permanent' applies to literature like never before.

Virtually every book that has ever been published is available on the internet.

And, while there is always room for new books, and the awards they attract, I do feel the book trade would benefit from dusting off the covers of the great works of literature and being more creative in promoting them to new audiences in new formats.

I wrote a column to this end which The Bookseller magazine published in 2007. If anything, because of technology, it is even more true today than it was then:

"At a family wedding last year, a cousin of mine from Washington DC told me that his favourite author is E. F. Benson. So last summer I read my first two Mapp and Lucia novels. They were published in 1920 and 1922. But they were new to me.

More recently, a friend told me that his favourite books are by Brian Moore. So, as this friend has invested money in my company Lovereading, I thought I should read Moore. It was called Colour of Blood and was written in 1987. But it was new to me (and, thanks John, I loved reading it).

Then I read that Sebastian Faulks considers 'Loving' by Henry Green the best novel ever written in the English language. So I definitely thought I should read that – even though it was written in 1945.

I bought all of these books very easily. As we all know, virtually every book that has ever been published is available on the internet. There are even book price comparison sites to find the cheapest place to buy the one you want. No problem.

This is how people buy books. Someone tells them about a good book and then they go and buy it. Sometimes these people have names like Richard or Judy. Sometimes the word, especially if it's Potter, gets round like wildfire and the book just takes off.

Yet the book trade doesn't work like this.

The book trade has things called 'frontlist' and 'backlist' titles.

Unlike every other market I have worked in, the new books – the ones that are really newsworthy – are 'promoted' as three-for-twos or even sold at half price. The old products, the ones that you might have thought had passed their sell-by date, the ones that may even be out of copyright, are mostly sold at full price on the high street. It's true – go to your nearest bookshop and see for yourself.

We all know about the effect of the major multiples on the book trade. But once you've been into your local bookshop, as requested above, pop into your nearest supermarket. Is the fresh, new crispy lettuce sold at half price with the older stuff still at full price? Of course not – that would be daft.

So there is massive potential value in 'backlist', and the best place for publishers to realise this value is on the internet. There are ways specialist bookshops could do it too.

But that is another story."

7
OFFICE POLITICS

7.1. THE AFFLICTION OF INTELLECTUALS WHO SEE ALL SIDES OF AN ARGUMENT

15 NOVEMBER 2011 08:52

Last week, I read the obituary of former Cabinet Minister, Sir Timothy Raison. He served under Edward Heath and Margaret Thatcher, apparently 'gaining a reputation as the keeper of the party's conscience on such issues as immigration, refugees, child benefit and social policy'. Bigots would instantly dismiss him as 'Tory'. To me, it seems he was a good man. My condolences to his friends and family.

One particular sentence in his obituary resonated with me:

'he suffered from that common affliction of intellectuals: the ability to see all sides of an argument'

Early in my career, I worked with people like this. They are not evil. Nor do they mean any harm. In fact, as Sir Timothy appears to have been, they may even be kind, considerate and well-meaning.

But they can be a nightmare to work with.

In my case, in advertising, the particular difficulty I faced when working with such people was, not only, that they could see all sides of an argument – but also, they could think of a good reason why any given piece of creative work was wrong.

De facto, if you can see all sides of every argument, you can see why something that might be right might also be wrong – so you may end up not doing anything at all. Leaders have to be 'smart' rather than intellectual.

On one occasion, with my 'upstream thinking' hat on, I was asked to try and rescue a brand, the account for which the client had put the agency on notice – quite deservedly too because this was a seasonal food product and, the previous year, the agency had failed to produce an approved script for the TV commercial our client expected.

No less than 71 scripts had been developed and rejected. Hard to believe but true.

This meant that not only had our client's brand failed to benefit from any advertising support during its crucial seasonal period (with a consequent lack of consumer demand and loss of distribution listings) but, most important, the agency missed out on the 15% commission that the management had included in their financial forecast to Head Office at the beginning of the year. Those were the days.

Worse, by now, such was the lack of morale and enthusiasm for this brand in the creative department, that unless drastic action was taken, our agency would never produce acceptable, let alone effective, advertising for this brand.

And our creatives were right. Every brand benefit had been explored from every angle and, for every script that had been developed, good reasons had been given for why it was not right. We were up the proverbial creek.

And the problem, I soon found out, was that the person providing these reasons was not the client but my very intellectual, kind, considerate and well-meaning boss.

I had to hope that a familiar dose of the old Hugh Salmon charisma would charm the creative department onto my side – at least for one more script.

Before bringing out the charm, and following my guru David Ogilvy's precedent on Dove decades before, I set to work finding out everything I could about the brand. I studied the research. I went to the factory. I joined a salesman on a day of trade visits. I even scored runs for that famous creative cricket team, the Box-Busters (these things are important when you need people on your side).

And guess what? I discovered one fact about our client's brand which, because it was a fact, could not be wrong. It was an undeniable, God's-honest-truth fact.

Furthermore, it was also a fact that none of our client's competitors could claim. It was unique. That was a fact too. In other words, my fact was not only a fact but also a unique fact (you have to spell things out clearly for these intellectual people).

So all we had to do now was convert the fact into a serious commercial proposition.

7.1. THE AFFLICTION OF INTELLECTUALS

And this our creative team was able to do. They developed a killer script.

A complete no-brainer.

But yes, you've guessed it, my intellectual boss found a reason it was wrong.

Although he agreed my discovery was a fact, he argued, would it make a good commercial?

This was when he was told, in no uncertain terms, that, by taking this position, he was putting at risk:

1. The market share of a famous brand
2. The agency's relationship with a prestigious client
3. And, worst of all, another year's income for our big bosses in Corporate HQ.

So the lesson is, if you find you have one of these formidably intelligent people holding your business back then, very kindly, you have to persuade this person that he or she might be in the wrong business – and, indeed, if they should be in business at all.

Back in the day, when I featured in the Campaign 'A List', they asked me for my 'Hates' and I said 'office politics and abominable no-men'.

When I said this, I didn't mean only those people you come across who have the corporate power to say 'no' but are not permitted to say 'yes' – and there are plenty of them around.

I was also thinking of this problem I had had of a boss who, like Sir Timothy Raison, was so intellectual that he could see all sides of every argument, including why we should not do anything at all.

Frankly, I do not think there is room for these people in the commercial world.

I believe, as a country, we are short of good teachers.

You may have one sitting in the office upstairs.

7.2. The Better You Do, the Worse It Gets

23 November 2011 08:44

Further to my last post where I showed how my boss was holding back the best interests of the company we were working for, there follows the human problem I have experienced of how to overcome this tricky situation.

You can find yourself placed in a 'no win' situation in terms of your own career.

You have two choices. You report the situation to someone even higher up the hierarchy, in which case your boss will feel betrayed. Or you confront your boss yourself.

Either way you are, in the vernacular, stuffed.

He or she will, at best, deny being the problem and, at worst, seek revenge.

In corporate life, this is not a good place to be. It means that however good a job you do, all credit will be whisked away. All of a sudden, any cock-ups by anyone else in the company will be your fault, even if you have been nowhere near the issue.

You are in a nightmare.

And the nightmare becomes even worse when you find your boss is sleeping with the boss on top.

If you find yourself in this position, please do not get angry.

This will only make things worse.

Your only option is to leave.

Ideally, with dignity.

7.3. When, even if you are right, you are wrong

5 December 2011 08:43

This is the last of my trilogy on what can happen if your boss gets in the way of your good work – and the consequences of his or her exacting revenge at the threat you have become.

The last line of my last post advised that if you have to leave, do so 'with dignity'.

You may have gathered that I speak from personal experience. In the world of work, what follows is the one lesson I would pass on to my kids. For those young people who, I gather, read this blog early in your careers, eager to succeed and keen to learn – this one is for you.

Having won the World Cup, in the face of what he felt was weak and inefficient management of the sport at HQ, the former England rugby coach, Sir Clive Woodward, felt he was in a strong position to determine the terms on which he would be prepared to maintain his role and improve the sport.

When his terms were rejected, he resigned.

In the subsequent press conference, he vented his spleen. He describes this event twenty six minutes into his fascinating appearance on the insightful radio show Desert Island Discs.

Subsequent events, right up to today, have shown that Woodward was right in what he was attempting to achieve but wrong to lose his cool at a press conference. As his wife told him, he burnt his bridges.

As I look back on my career, I have been guilty of this too. I have not left well.

On one occasion, where my company did not deliver on promises made to me and attempted, rather pathetically, to weasel out of firm agreements made, I lost faith in an agency to which I had given my heart and soul for a number of years.

I resigned.

Further, I took it upon myself to write an analysis of the wrongs that had been done to me, the flaws of the London management team and the changes needed to improve the management of the agency. I predicted that if the agency did not take notice of what I was saying, its reputation and performance would suffer.

I sent my views to HQ and cc'd the London management team at which they were aimed.

I came across this memo the other day. And I cringed.

I cringed because, even though every one of the points I made have subsequently been proved right, I was wrong to make them. I burnt my bridges.

Because of this, although not one of the individuals I pinpointed are there now, there is very little chance of my going back, however much I would love to do so.

If I had left with dignity – reputation and integrity intact – who knows?

So, if ever you are shafted by shallow office politicians, stabbed in the back by those around you, plotted against by an inadequate boss, please remember you have read this post, listen again to Sir Clive Woodward on Desert Island Discs, bite your tongue and keep the behavioural high ground.

I promise, in the end, you will be better off.

7.4. WHEN YOUR GREATEST STRENGTH IS YOUR GREATEST WEAKNESS

31 AUGUST 2012 08:57

I saw my doctor yesterday. Sensitive, intelligent, considerate, thoughtful and understanding, he is as kind a man as any I have met.

But I have a problem with him.

So kind, sensitive, intelligent, considerate, thoughtful and understanding is he that he always runs over time. While he attends to the patient he is tending, the patients in the waiting room wait and wait and wait. This can be most annoying.

In this way, what pleases me most about my brilliant doctor is what annoys me most.

Do you see what I mean?

A few years ago, we employed a graduate who wanted to be in advertising. She was (and, I guess, still is) kind, sensitive, intelligent, considerate, thoughtful and understanding. She loved her work and we loved working with her. On discussing any issue, she always 'got it' and made smart, useful contributions to the debate.

Further, whenever discussions were over, and she wrote the meeting notes, not only did they accurately reflect what had been said but she would add a little bit more, something extra, to the matter at hand. Often, this was something that she had been too shy to say face-to-face.

Shy? Yes, she was shy. In fact, so kind, sensitive, intelligent, considerate, thoughtful and understanding was she that when I asked her to get things done, she would shy away. She would rather do something herself than get other people, especially suppliers, to do things for her, especially if price was an issue.

In this way, her kind, sensitive, intelligent, considerate, thoughtful and understanding nature was the very thing that frustrated us most when we depended on her to get things done, on budget, and on time.

Do you see where I'm heading?

I hope so because things are about to get more serious.

Not long ago, I worked with a guy who turned out to be a crook. Of course, when I started working with him, I did not know he was a crook. But now I know what I know, I am going to remember this theme and keep my eyes open for people like him.

What do I mean?

Well, it emerged that this guy was an expert at reading contracts. You may not think this a particular talent.

But it is.

In fact, there are people whose entire careers involve the insertion of sneaky traps into long, tedious legal contracts. The most obvious example is a sneaky clause, hidden in the small print of a big document, that says if you don't do this by then, the contract becomes null and void and the other side gets all the money.

Well, this guy I worked with was very good at spotting these sneaky traps. It was a particular strength of his. And, of course, that which made him identify sneaky clauses in contracts was that which enabled him to insert sneaky clauses into contracts himself. In this way, he squeezed much more out of our client than the client thought he was giving us – none of it to do with the quality of the work or results we achieved. Just the way the contract was written. And this guy had drafted it.

You can guess what happened. Yes, not only had this guy slipped sneaky clauses into our client contract, but he slipped a sneaky clause into his contract with me.

It directly contradicted what we had agreed.

Trusting as I am, I had overlooked it.

Luckily, I found him out after he had stolen money from me and the dishonest contract was nullified.

Phew.

In this way, what this guy is good at makes him very bad news for the rest of mankind.

People.

Not easy are they?

8
SPORT

8.1. When all you can do is play the ball bowled to you

31 August 2014 11:45

To many of us, especially those of us who lived through those days, the TV series *Mad Men* has been essential viewing. We have come to know the character Don Draper, played by John Hamm, like a friend. And now, this week, Hamm's new film *Million Dollar Arm* has come to London. And it's about cricket! Wahaay! Have the Americans seen the light?

Now, if you don't play cricket, I am sorry. Please bear with me. Who knows, the lesson in this post might change your life, just as a cricket ball can end it.

For, if you do play cricket, you will know that batting is a dangerous pastime. And it can be a mental disaster. It's ok once you are 'in' and have scored some runs. You have become used to the pace of the pitch, experienced the speed and guile of the bowlers and mapped the positioning of the fielders. The longer you bat, the more relaxed you become.

But, every time you bat, your first ball is a nightmare. As you stand there, nervously watching the bowler charging towards you, you have no idea what to expect or whether you will be up to the task ahead.

No one has said anything or done anything to you.

Nor have you done anything to them.

Your only job is to stand and look. But your brain is scrambled. You wonder if your feet are in the right place, your knees sufficiently bent, your back straight, your head at the right angle, the bat in your hands pointing in the right direction and your eyes are working.

Sometimes, it seems your eyes are not working at all.

For there are times, as I myself can testify, when your first ball is unleashed at you at such a ferocious pace that, quite simply, you do not see it.

There is the whirling of a white-clothed human being twenty two yards ahead of you; a blurred vision of something red rocketing towards your face and whooshing past your nose; an eerie, evil whirr as the seam of the ball rotates and hurtles through the whistling air; and a sharp smack as it bullets into the gloves of the wicket-keeper behind you.

Then comes the humiliation of a knowing, gloating, smirking, superior guffaw from the fielders as they confirm something you thought only you knew.

You haven't seen the ball at all.

Then, horror of horrors, within a minute, in less than sixty seconds, the same thing, the same sheer terror, will be unleashed at you again. To the amateur player, the village cricketer, the brain becomes more scrambled, the self-doubt more exaggerated, the fear more extreme. Will the next ball be as fast as the last? Will it hit me? Should I take a different stance? Stand further back in the crease? Get my head straighter? Raise my bat less far in the backlift? Was that last ball really that quick? What if I don't see it again?

What am I doing here?

Professional cricketers, people who are really good at batting, who know what they are doing, who, perhaps, have got their head together, are different. They don't have these feelings of self-doubt. Whether by nature or training or both, they have the ability, and the mental strength, to put the last ball behind them.

What has just happened will have no impact on what is about to happen.

They wipe it from the memory.

It is in the past.

Gone.

Good cricketers play the ball that is bowled to them.

This summer, one of my oldest and closest friends, and as it happens one of the best cricketers I have played with, was not appointed to a job on which he had set his heart. He works in a place where he has dedicated his entire working life. For the last few years, he has been a worthy and successful number two in the batting order.

Now, on the retirement of the number one, many of us who are stakeholders in this business justifiably expected him to progress smoothly and seamlessly into the top spot. And with this important job would come respect, status, a feeling of achievement, of a life well spent.

8.1. WHEN ALL YOU CAN DO IS PLAY THE BALL BOWLED TO YOU

But my friend missed out. Another guy was selected. Someone from outside the business. Someone none of us know or, frankly, care about. Now, I must not be unfair to this guy. I wasn't on the selection panel or part of the process.

It may be he is a worthy candidate. Indeed it must be.

He may have qualities I have not seen. Indeed he must have.

But he is new.

And 'new' is a risk, isn't it? It must be.

It never ceases to amaze me how often this happens, how few leaders of organisations 'grow their own successor', as my advertising guru David Ogilvy used to say. No mad man he.

Soon after I started my career at his agency, then known as Ogilvy & Mather, our chairman retired. His successor, Peter Warren, who had worked for Ogilvy man-and-boy, having started in the post room, eased himself seamlessly into the chair. Michael Baulk, also Ogilvy man-and-boy, smoothed into the role of Managing Director.

Baulk and Warren became the dream team. So much so that they were poached by Abbott Mead Vickers – still, twenty years later as AMV BBDO, the biggest advertising agency in London.

I remember being amazed that O&M let this happen.

I suspect it must have been something to do with share options or performance bonuses, but someone let them go. At what price? Why grow your own talent all the way to the top and then let it slip away, as has just happened to my friend? This, surely, is madness.

For, needless to say, O&M replaced Baulk and Warren with 'outside' appointments who in the eyes of many, not least me, were a disaster.

A unique corporate culture that had been grown and nurtured and cherished over decades disappeared down the Thames.

And what about the big wide world outside advertising? Next year, after the General Election, how many of the new Cabinet will be qualified to become ministers of government? What, for example, if a deal has to be done with UKIP? Will these appointments be made on merit or political expediency? Or will these people have been grown, nurtured, into their jobs? I think we know the answer.

So what of my friend?

I can't help feeling a mistake has been made. But this won't help him will it? In terms of the top job, he has been given 'out'.

And, as my dad used to say, once you're out, you're out.

However, while many of us moan and groan from our fielding positions of ignorance on the outside of this decision, and knowing him as I do, my friend's stance will be solid, his bat straight, his head held high, his eyes focused on the track ahead …

… and he will play the next ball that is bowled to him.

And this, let me tell you, is greatness.

8.2. Digital media, rugby and gutless management

4 MARCH 2011 09:13

If you don't know anything about rugby, it is a team game with 15 players a side. Two are 'centres' (unless you are in New Zealand, which we are not).

In the 1980s, aeons before today's digital media age, my brother played centre for England against Scotland. The other centre was Simon Halliday. I was there.

Neither of them was passed the ball all game, so neither had the chance to drop it.

Neither of them missed a tackle or made any other mistake. England were thrashed. The following week, Simon telephoned Jamie and said:

'Have you seen Teletext today?'

'No. Why?' Jamie replied.

'We've both been dropped', said Simon.

'Why?' asked Jamie.

'No idea'.

A few weeks later, Simon called Jamie again:

'Have you seen Teletext today?'

'No. Why?'

'We're both back in the team'.

'Why?'

'No idea'.

In those days, as you may gather from the above, rugby was an amateur sport. Rugby players had 'proper' jobs. Even so, as young men playing in front of large crowds and with mass media attention upon them, this treatment must have hurt.

Could not someone have picked up the phone and spoken to them man-to-man?

More recently, Sir Clive Woodward was on Desert Island Discs. He said when he was centre for England, he could not believe the shambolic management he experienced. It was a complete contrast to his day job in the aggressive sales force at Rank Xerox.

Years later, as England manager in a newly professional game, Woodward resolved to develop a more professional management approach. His team won the World Cup.

Arise, Sir Clive.

Anyway, last week, Jamie and I are having dinner and he has a very black and white view of how people communicate by email, text, Facebook and Twitter these days.

Indeed, as the only rugby player to have been capped for New Zealand and England (another story), some might think he is entitled to a black and white view of life.

Having been a television presenter, written a weekly national newspaper column and now working with a successful sports PR agency, Jamie knows the game.

And, perhaps because of his own heartless, hurtful experience as a young man, he feels very strongly that people should either meet face-to-face or at least pick up the phone and talk to each other more – especially when the business equivalent of being 'dropped' is the issue.

And I agree with him wholeheartedly.

In my view …

… if you are a client who fires an agency by email, text or other Faceless manner

… or

… an agency manager who fires an employee by email, text or other Faceless manner

… you are a gutless coward.

8.3. WHAT POLITICIANS COULD LEARN FROM RUGBY (AND THE MARINES)

16 AUGUST 2011 08:20

Next week, Martin Johnson, the manager of the England rugby team, has to cut his current squad of 40 players down to the final 30 who will travel to New Zealand for the forthcoming World Cup.

A few years ago, I attended a lunch at which Sir Clive Woodward was guest speaker. He was the England manager for the World Cups of 1999 and 2003 and was faced with the same decision then as Martin Johnson faces next week.

Sir Clive spoke very eloquently on the subject of leadership, teamwork and human behaviour.

I cannot quote him verbatim, but one of his lessons was particularly interesting.

In 1997, he took his 40-man squad down to the Headquarters of the Royal Marines for a 'beasting' (vernacular for intense physical training).

In a series of carefully worked out challenges and alien situations, the England rugby squad would be tested on the importance of teamwork in waging war and killing people. In this context, their rugby could only improve.

Woodward's story went something like this:

After the beasting, which all agreed had been a punishing but eye-opening experience, he wrote and thanked the Colonel of the Regiment for his kind hospitality.

A few days later, he realised he had not thanked the Sergeant Major, the guy who had actually done all the work and taught his players some life-changing lessons.

So Woodward gave him a call to thank him and then, almost as an afterthought, he asked him if he agreed with his final selection of 30 of the initial 40-man squad.

"Well" said the Sergeant Major "I've been a football supporter all my life. I'm a Millwall man through and through. I don't know anything about rugby. But I have to tell you that you have picked three men who we would not go to war with".

"What do you mean?" said Woodward, shocked and concerned.

"Well, sir, I don't know if these three guys are good rugby players or not. I don't know if they have superior skills to the others or if they make better decisions under pressure than some you have left behind.

But, in the Marines, we know there are certain people in life who live for themselves and only themselves.

They are more interested in their own good, not the success of the team. If something goes wrong, it is someone else's fault. If they see themselves in competition with a colleague, they will undermine that person by making snide comments behind their back or lobbying others against them.

They are not capable of taking personal responsibility for their own actions.

They suck attention from those around them and don't give anything back.

We call them energy-sappers".

In 1997, it was too late for Woodward to change his final squad.

England were knocked out in the quarter-finals.

In 2003, Woodward remembered the words of the Sergeant Major.

There were no energy-sappers in the squad.

England won the World Cup.

8.4. Being English, British and European in Sport

30 September 2010 23:01

We are a sporting nation. Or are we?

Sport, unlike Christianity (unless the Pope is here – see last post 4.6), benefits from ubiquitous media coverage. The lives of our sports stars are ruthlessly exposed (unless they can help it).

Today, as if you didn't know, it is the Ryder Cup – in which 'we' are Europe.

On Sunday, it is the Commonwealth Games, in which 'we' are – individually – England, Scotland, Wales and Northern Ireland.

In 2012, it is the Olympic Games – in which 'we' will be Great Britain.

Except we won't be.

Not in football, anyway.

From what I have gathered from Sky News (a paywall free online news channel):

'The Scottish, Welsh and Irish Football Associations have privately agreed to turn a blind eye to a one-off British team for the Olympic Games. In return for their co-operation it is thought that the English FA will not ask players outside England to join the team. The agreement should put an end to an argument which has raged since 2005, when London won the right to stage the Olympics. Scotland, Wales and Northern Ireland have been against the idea for fear it would set a dangerous precedent and jeopardise their independence in future competitions.'

Why don't we play as Great Britain in the biggest tournament of all – the football World Cup?

Well, having been lucky enough to have witnessed the inside of international sport in my time, I can tell you.

What happens is that each of the four regions that make up Great Britain – England, Scotland, Wales and Northern Ireland – have a Committee. These Committees are very important with very important people on them. And they are allocated privileged tickets to World Cups, even if the 'country' they represent doesn't qualify.

So, if we entered the World Cup as Great Britain, only a quarter of the men in suits and their fur-coated wives would get their four-yearly five-star treatment.

What must the other countries, each with their own cultural divisions, think?

Spain – which includes proud Catalans, Basques and Galicians – won the World Cup this year.

CNN reported:

'Many of this morning's newspapers in Spain have hinted that the victory could herald a new dawn for the country, where a sense of national identity might now take precedence over regional concerns…The transformative power of football, either by promoting national unity or through sparking a long-dormant national pride… has been known to have huge political significance.'

Wouldn't it have been great if Ryan Giggs, Kenny Dalglish and George Best had had the opportunity to play more competitively on the world stage?

Sadly, it seems the only way this will happen in football is if, one day, which may be soon upon us, we are so bad that Great Britain will have to unite as one to compete with other nations of the world.

Just as Britain became Europe to compete with the USA in the Ryder Cup.

So, whatever happens this week-end in Wales, or next week in India, we can look forward to our media being as one-eyed as they always are, whoever 'we' are.

Just you watch.

9
MUSIC & POETRY

9.1. If you can whistle, you're not tone deaf

24 March 2014 08:40

My late father's only sister, my Aunt Hetty, died last month.

My earliest memories of Aunt Hetty are of Kenya and a different world. For the first 17 years of my life, 'home' was Hong Kong where I was born. From the age of nine, I was sent away from home to a godforsaken Roman Catholic boarding school near a maggot factory in Nottinghamshire. Not the happiest days of my life. In fact, the most miserable.

One summer, my father announced that, rather than fly straight from Hong Kong to school in England, he had arranged for me to stop off in Kenya on the way. As you do. I was fifteen.

There cannot be a much greater contrast than Hong Kong and Kenya. One, a tiny island crammed with five million people, the other offering mile after mile of pure, natural, African beauty.

In Kenya, people would drive a hundred miles to go to a party. In Hong Kong, you would be in communist China if you did that. Or adrift in the Pacific Ocean.

In Kenya, my uncle managed a coffee plantation for a wealthy landowner. In Hong Kong, my father worked for a shipping company. Both men had fought a war for their country and were now getting by on whatever life offered them in the outposts of what used to be the British Empire.

Aunt Hetty was a brave, strong, forceful lady – as, perhaps, you need to be to survive in Africa – and she had a loud, hearty, infectious laugh which her three daughters seem to have inherited.

Poignantly, at her memorial service, we heard how heartbroken, as a teenager, she had been at the death of her younger brother. Hugh Salmon was killed at the age of 17 in the explosive sinking of HMS Barham on 25 November 1941. I was named in his memory.

Nowadays, it is easy for us to forget how young many of our oldest living compatriots were when they lost their parents and brothers and sisters. Now in their eighties and nineties, they have suffered – mostly in silence – for a long time, haven't they?

It is fair to say that, in one particular way, Aunt Hetty changed my life.

One day, it may have been in Kenya, she asked me if I was learning to play a musical instrument.

No, I was not.

Did I sing in a choir?

No, I didn't.

Really? Not sing at all?

No, Aunt Hetty. I am tone deaf.

That can't be true, she said. You come from a musical family. You can't be tone deaf. Can you whistle?

No.

Whistle for me.

I can't do that!

Yes, you can. Go on. Whistle . Did I say she was forceful?

I whistled Colonel Bogey.

'There you are!' she said. 'That was perfect. You're not tone deaf at all!'

And, do you know, my life has been much richer for knowing that.

Little things mean a lot, don't they?

RIP.

9.2. THE WAY FORWARD FOR ROCK BANDS

18 DECEMBER 2009 13:15

Early in my career, a rock band asked me to be their manager. I listened to their demo and was impressed but, for various reasons, I was more than a little underwhelmed by the music business at the time.

And I had one big doubt in my mind. This band did not want to play live. They just wanted to be a studio band. As their potential manager, I knew that this would be a dangerous way forward. Actually, I thought it would restrict their potential to make money, which I wanted them to do (so I could take a cut for myself), but this didn't seem to matter to the band. They just wanted to sit in a studio, get stoned and make great music.

Luckily, I knew the Managing Director of Island Records. He agreed to meet for a beer one lunchtime. We did that kind of thing in those days.

He told me something very interesting and I have never forgotten it. He said the Island Records philosophy was very simple.

If a band was big in Dublin and if, every week, more and more fans turned up to see them, Island would encourage the band to go and play in Belfast.

If, then, more and more fans turned up to see them in Belfast, they would encourage and, by this time, pay for them to play in Cardiff – and then Leicester, then Manchester, then London and then the world.

Of course, he was talking about U2.

In fact, at the time of our beer (or three), he told me Island Records were out of pocket to U2 to the tune of nearly a million pounds – and those were the days when a million quid was worth a flipping lot more than an MP's house.

But Island Records knew four things:

1. They knew that wherever U2 played, they would build an audience.

2. They knew that if U2's music was popular in one country, it would be popular in the next country.

3. They knew that U2 were young and hungry and just wanted to play live music to live people – every night if possible. Gigs were their passion.

4. And the last thing Island knew was that if, wherever they went, U2 could pack out pubs and clubs and stadiums, then Island could sell a lot of records for U2 (and take a cut for themselves).

And so I went back to my mates and told them that my career as manager of a rock band was over before it had started.

And the band never made it either.

No gig-time, no big-time (sorry).

But I have never forgotten this very important lesson. I guess you could call it 'bottom up' rather than 'top down' marketing.

However, in this digital age, is this lesson relevant any more?

Certainly, the music market has been turned upside down. Now, bands give away their 'records' for free online. Then, when the music has become popular, more fans will go and see them live – and, proportionately, pay much more to do so. Plus, of course, there is that highly-marked-up stuff called merchandising.

And, actually, the fans get a better deal this way. Because they have had access to the music for free, they know all the songs the bands play live.

In the old days, in order to hear the tracks you did want to hear, you had to endure half a gig of music from the band's new album which, because you had not been given the chance to get to like it, made you feel a bit ripped off – but it was the only way the band could get their new music 'out there'.

So, way back then, the band played all the gigs they could by way of launching their new music and made money from selling 'records'. Now, they give you the new music for nothing and make money from the gigs – which tend to be staged smarter, more expensive, 'named' venues with more expensive, drinks, food and T-shirts.

U2 @ O2 (sorry again).

However, every rule has exceptions.

As we have seen over the last few weeks, the massive TV exposure created by The X Factor has created awareness very quickly for a small amount of people – this way, Cowell will coin it in even more when he starts selling these people's records before they start playing live. The sheer volume of the OFFLINE exposure has paid massive dividends.

9.2. THE WAY FORWARD FOR ROCK BANDS

But in Susan Boyle's case it was the explosion of one simple video clip of her first TV appearance online that created her worldwide following.

So where does this leave us in the real world?

Since my Island Records U2 lesson, I have always challenged clients and agencies (both creative and media) not to think:

"what is the best way of spending the budget we have been given?"

but:

"if our budget was a thousand pounds rather than, say a million pounds, what would we do and can we build a more effective campaign from the bottom up rather than from our budget down?"

I am certain that however many media channels we can access, however great the online explosion and however much data we can access and track, this is a factor worth considering more than ever.

9.3. Why You Would Be a Mug to Be a Poet

19 June 2014 23:30

I have met people who are very, very rich.
    I have met people who are famous.
    I have met great sportsmen.
    I have met academics.
    I have met aristocrats.
    I have met celebrities.
    I have met film stars.
    I have met singers.
    I have met bands.
    Even royalty.
    But the people I admire most are writers.

Thus, at Ogilvy & Mather, at the start of my advertising career, it was the words, the time and the company of the poet Edwin Brock that provided some of my most treasured moments. Several times, we shared train journeys to our client in the Midlands. I didn't say much. I just listened. He gave me a signed book of his poems. Unforgivably, I've lost it.

Brock's poem Five Ways to Kill a Man has been described as 'one of the best-known poems of the last century'. What must he have felt while he was crafting copy for an ad – only for it to be manhandled and defaced by ignorant, pig-headed, besuited managers like me?

Now, in 2014, we are celebrating the centenary of the birth of Dylan Thomas and, although his birthday was 27 October, I have caught three Dylan Thomas television programmes already:

On 18 May, there was the 'intoxicating' (sic) BBC drama A Poet In New York.

On 31 May, we had The Poetry of Dylan Thomas, 'a special centenary celebration reading of the work of the great Welsh poet' at the Hay Festival.

9.3. WHY YOU WOULD BE A MUG TO BE A POET

And on 1 June, in a programme called Dylan Thomas – A Poet's Guide, Owen Sheers made 'the case for Dylan Thomas being one of the major poets of the 20th Century: a visionary and a craftsman.'

To me, the most remarkable revelation in this last programme was, after he had left a prodigious youth behind, quite how few poems Dylan Thomas wrote. And how broke he was. And how miserable.

And how much of his work do we remember today? Richard Burton's reading of Under Milk Wood must be one of the most skilful artistic creations of our time. There is Fern Hill and Do Not Go Gentle Into That Good Night and And Death Shall Have No Dominion.

But how many people know how many more of the man's great works?

And how was the life of Dylan Thomas?

You don't have to be a cricket fan like me to be moved by these words of the great John Arlott:

'I worshipped Dylan. I thought he was a great poet and a great reader. I thought he was a lovely man. And when he died, I wept… I did get a letter from him not long before the end saying 'Dear John, I need a lot of money. I don't want it all from you. I was going to say £20 but send me £10. I'm not going to promise to pay it back because I never shall. But if you don't want to send it you needn't.' Thank God I sent it. It was the last time I ever heard from him. If ever I thought a man had a touch of divinity, it was Dylan.'

How sad is that? How tragic.

And this, remember, is one of the greatest poets of all time. A man whose work, even if only a handful of poems, will live forever. A man with immortality. 'A touch of divinity' no less.

Earlier this month, and rather controversially, the broadcaster Jeremy Paxman said this:

'I think poetry has really rather connived at its own irrelevance and that shouldn't happen… It seems to me very often that poets now seem to be talking to other poets and that is not talking to people as a whole.'

I think Paxman is right.

I spent a short time of my career in the music business. Like I said, I have met singers and bands.

And do you know what drives the lives of these people?

It is a thing called royalties.

Every time their work, their creative expression, is played, these people take a cut. Most often, they fall out with each other because one of them takes more of a cut than the others. Litigation, jealousy and greed ensue.

And so does lots and lots of money.

The royalties business is highly sophisticated. There are royalties on the writing of the music and the lyrics. There are royalties on airplay and performance. There are royalties on the production. There are even royalties on the material on which the material is produced (tape, vinyl, MP3 file etc).

As with musicians and singers, some actors get royalties – including, as I know to the cost of my clients, if they appear in advertisements.

You only have to write one great song and you will receive an income for life. In the 1960s, a guy called Reg Presley wrote a song called Love is All Around. Apparently it took him all of 10 minutes. In 1994, the song was chosen as the feature song for the movie Four Weddings and a Funeral. Reg earned 'massive royalties'. And then, in 2003, the song was featured in the movie Love Actually and – oh what joy! – even more royalties!

Let me tell you, the writer Reg Presley led a far, far richer life than the writer Dylan Thomas.

I have always felt it strange that sportsmen do not get royalties. At one time, I knew George Best a bit. Did he get royalties every time his brilliant goals were shown on TV? Did he heck. He was nearly as broke as Dylan Thomas.

And do royalty get royalties? Does Her Majesty get a cut whenever her coronation is shown? Do her offspring get a farthing from any of the photographs of them that are beamed and published around the world? No, they do not.

So, if Edwin Brock had been thirty years younger than me rather than thirty years older than me, would I have advised him to earn his crust by writing advertising copy at the behest of people like me?

The heck I would.

Alongside his poetry writing, I would advise him, implore him, to write lyrics and, just like the 'highest paid poet in the world' Bernie Taupin (estimated wealth £180m), send them to Elton John (estimated wealth £220m).

And if Edwin did not have the contacts to do this, and time had spun on a different axis, he could have given his lyrics to Elton John's civil partner David Furnish.

He worked at Ogilvy & Mather too.

10
MEDIA

10.1. SUPER-INJUNCTIONS, CONTRA MUNDUM ORDERS AND SOCIAL MEDIA

26 April 2011 08:07

It is a weird feeling when someone you know becomes the talk of the moment. This happened to me last week (no sorry, I don't know Prince William or Kate Middleton).

Mr Justice Eady issued a Contra Mundum super-injunction to prevent publication of 'intimate photographs' of a married public figure, whom we are to call OPQ, after a woman tried to sell them for a 'large sum of money'.

A Contra Mundum super-injunction is 'enforceable worldwide and in perpetuity'.

'Amoral judges, shameless celebrities and a Britain that's coming close to a police state' railed The Mail.

'Blame the gagging judges, not the Human Rights Act' pronounced The Telegraph.

'At the rate the judge is going, I'm surprised he didn't make the order to cover the whole solar system' said helpful Liberal Democrat MP John Hemming.

Now I know Sir David Eady.

At one time, I alleged that lies had been told about me to cover up a financial fraud I had discovered as Managing Director of CM:Lintas, a subsidiary of Interpublic.

David Eady QC was my barrister in this action. I believe mine was his last case as a QC before becoming a High Court judge. (In defamation, words like 'I believe', 'I think', 'in my view' are very important).

So here are three facts:

1. On 3 April 1997, Lintas Worldwide issued a Public Statement:

'Hugh Salmon was employed by CM Lintas International Limited ("CMLI") as Managing Director from June to October 1992. During his brief spell with that

company he brought successful management disciplines into the company and showed a thorough knowledge of the advertising industry. He worked hard and constructively to advance CMLI's interests.

In the event, Mr Salmon was dismissed from the Company by Chris Munds, the Chairman of CMLI. That dismissal was wrongful and he was compensated for that wrongful dismissal.

Since then, Mr Salmon has taken further proceedings against Chris Munds, CMLI and Lintas Worldwide ("Lintas") and those proceedings have very recently been settled in circumstances where substantial compensation has been paid to Mr Salmon.

Lintas accept that Mr Salmon was respected by clients and staff and that his career has been severely affected by untrue suggestions to the contrary for which Lintas apologise to Mr Salmon. Lintas further accept that Mr Salmon was justified in bringing these proceedings and they wish him well in the future.'

2. On 11 April 1997, the front page of Campaign magazine said:

'Interpublic Group is facing one of the biggest legal bills in British advertising history after a sensational climbdown...'

3. A leader article in the same issue of Campaign said:

'Lintas has offered no explanation of such activity; whether or not it was authorised, whether action is to be taken against any individuals or whether any client suffered'.

So there was a time when my life, in a way, depended on David Eady.

And I can say, from a depth of personal experience that I doubt (sic) any of these journalists or MPs have had of him, that David Eady is not only one of the most formidably intelligent men I have met, but also a deeply compassionate, caring man who is determined for right to win over wrong.

He also has a deep respect for the law. Time after time, in meeting after meeting, he overrode advertising people like me and Rupert Howell, who had agreed to be my 'expert witness', and directed our emotional opinions to the rational letter of the law.

And, I have to tell you, David Eady knows what he is talking about.

I have no doubt whatsoever that, in the case of OPQ, Mr Justice Eady was applying his extraordinary brain to interpreting and applying the law. If Article 8 of the Human Rights Convention (which upholds the right to privacy and to which our politicians have signed up) is written in such a way as Mr Justice Eady is required to make a ruling, then he will do

10.1. SUPER-INJUNCTIONS, CONTRA MUNDUM ORDERS

so based on his interpretation of that law and not on his own personal prejudices. I do not care what any journalists or MPs say. Believe me.

Why are my own experience in defamation and this 'Contra Mundum' order relevant to the marketing and media world?

Well, the first is to establish that I might know a bit about the law of defamation and the second lies in the explanation of the phrase 'Contra Mundum' above:

'A Contra Mundum order is enforceable worldwide and in perpetuity'.

But is it?

By which I mean, is it enforceable?

I believe, for all his knowledge of the law, that marketing experts might know what they are talking about here more than Mr Justice Eady – although I do not know this for sure because Twitter was not around when I knew him. Please note the careful use of language in this paragraph.

As an industry, we know about the extraordinary impact of Twitter, Facebook and the internet generally.

We also know about the huge financial valuations that are currently being placed on these and other 'new media' companies. We are experiencing another dotcom boom.

These valuations are based on the value of these potential audiences in terms of marketing and advertising cash.

One issue of concern is the anonymity, inanity – and, now, legality – of many of the comments made on the internet. They are certainly a consideration to advertisers backing the sites that 'distribute' or 'broadcast' them (deliberate 'old media' terms).

So when a Contra Mundum order is issued in London, it raises a debate and a set of questions that our industry has a vested interest in answering:

- to what extent, in the real world, is this Contra Mundum enforceable?
- why is it easier to defame someone online rather than offline?
- what about all these 'comments' that are made behind a veil of anonymity?
- are these anonymous commentators above the law?
- if so, why?
- if not, to what extent are they controllable?
- what are we doing to police them?
- what are the owners of websites and blogging forums doing to monitor them?

- is there a code of practice?

- should advertisers support websites that do not abide by a code of practice?

- who is making the rules?

For what it is worth I believe, as an industry, we should be doing far more than we are to take a lead on these issues.

In particular, with their worldwide knowledge of consumers and new media trends, multi-national companies and agency groups can make a massive contribution. After all, it is their budgets upon which these worldwide websites will depend for revenue.

If nothing else, we need an agreed Code of Practice (the 'Contra Mundum Code'?) where online companies should build in checks whereby the people who make comments on their sites are identifiable in person – and answerable to the law.

If websites don't know who their customers are, then I don't think advertisers should pay to reach them.

I believe advertisers, and agencies that act for them, should be lobbying politicians to develop ways of enforcing people to behave online in just the same way as they do offline – by law.

And politicians would be far better off making better laws for today's world than taking cheap personal shots at the judges who have to interpret them.

10.2. How the Beeb blew it

4 December 2009 14:37

Don't any of these highly paid BBC executives or flipping MPs understand just how much £142.50 means to people in the real world out there?

Actually, I mean the real Britain, not the real world. In fact, that's my point.

When CNN was launched in 1980, it had had almost zero content. Now it is a massive worldwide media powerhouse. And, in those far off days of 1990, do you know what content viewers were prepared to sign up to?

Well, I can tell you. In some parts of the world, such was CNN's dearth of content, and so desperate was CNN to expand globally, that viewers in say, Asia, were prepared to sign up and pay for the CNN weather forecast for yesterday in Florida from the day before yesterday.

Get that? On a Wednesday in Asia, people would watch the weather forecast from the previous Monday for what the weather would be in Florida on Tuesday, the day before they were viewing this 'forecast'. Why would people, sweating in Hong Kong or freezing on Mount Fuji, pay for that? But they did.

And, more importantly, how on earth did the BBC ever allow this to happen? How did the BBC even allow CNN to take off at all, let alone for Ted Turner to laugh all the way to the bank and into Jane Fonda's arms?

I'll tell you why. It was because of the licence fee.

The BBC management never had to worry about revenue, never had to bother about the sheer hunger for news and entertainment from billions of people with billions of televisions and radios, never had to think about the explosion in world markets with worldwide corporations and worldwide brands and certainly never saw that, one day, there might be a worldwide web of people with a world vision.

They just sat there – myopically – in Regent Street or Shepherd's Bush and 'earned' their fat salaries based on their entirely forecastable revenue that was being provided by taxing the relatively small number of Brits who were forced to pay for these short-sighted people.

And, all this time, which of the BBC and CNN had a worldwide reputation, largely through the World Service, for editorial integrity, expert journalism and trust?

And which of the BBC and CNN had a catalogue of content of such outstanding creative quality that they are still repeating it to this day?

The answer, of course, is the BBC.

Remember, we are talking about all of the programming ever produced by the BBC up to 1980 versus CNN with virtually no content at all.

Because of this, CNN's very existence is a national disgrace to the British people. We should be ashamed of ourselves.

So what can we do about it?

Well, there is only one answer. Punish these BBC wasters by setting them a commercial challenge that – if they cannot fulfil – will force them to take their fat pensions and fast forward themselves off somewhere else. They should be ashamed to show their faces in the High Streets of Britain.

Right now, they have a strategy to save money and be more politically correct by moving a chunk of their business to Manchester. What do their potential audience in India and China and the whole wide world care about that? We are talking about an audience of billions here.

It gets worse.

According to Campaign Live last week, "The BBC is considering floating a portion of BBC Worldwide, its commercial arm, following increased pressure from the government and commercial rivals to reduce its media market power…the company is reported to be holding talks with City advisers regarding the issue as part of a strategic review of its worldwide entity, which is estimated to have a total equity value of £2 billion."

Billions of people – and now billions of pounds?!

And, in all this, the BBC still wants a few million Brits, many of whom are struggling like never before, to cough up £142.50 a year to fund this madness.

Get this – £142.50 is double the dole of increasing numbers of our people – and, to some, over a month of their disability allowance.

What on earth is going on?

10.2. HOW THE BEEB BLEW IT

Here is one solution. The UK taxpayer should set the BBC a limit of five years to reduce the licence fee to nothing by that time. As a sop, they should be allowed to sell advertising on a commercial basis except on BBC 2, BBC Radio and BBC World Service. After that, they should be set a target of paying corporation tax on profits at competitive market levels so that some of this £2 billion can be returned to the hands that have fed this antiquated and myopic anachronism for so long.

I don't care about the execution but it must be right that the strategic objective must be to force the BBC to face the commercial realities of the big, wide world out there and stop bleeding the poor people in the UK to enrich yet another bunch of 'City advisers' and entertain audiences around the globe.

It is the UK taxpayer who deserves – at last – to receive the BBC for free.

It is time for the rest of the world to pay us for that privilege.

And it is the human responsibility of the BBC's management to make this happen.

10.3. Humanity can overcome technology

14 February 2012 21:26

Two days. Two media channels. Two writers.

Alain de Botton is an eminent philosopher who has written 'How Proust Can Change Your Life', 'The Consolations of Philosophy' and 'The Pleasures and Sorrows of Work'. Last week, he tweeted:

'What used to happen to outrage before the net gave it a home?'

Charles Vallance is the V, some say the brains, of VCCP – anointed last week as 'the most 'in-demand' shop' (viz advertising agency) in London. Last week, he published a column in Campaign magazine headed:

'The web is stifling radicalism at a time when it is needed.'

Two clever geezers. What are they on about?

In their different ways, they both ask the same question. Vallance, unconstrained by 140 characters, developed his answer:

'What is the punk of today or, even, the Thatcherism? Where are the Marmite and the polarity? The most recent counter movement ... has been led by the geeks. While the internet has had a revolutionary impact on autocratic regimes, in the free world it seems to have had an opposite, almost sedative, effect. The incessant sharing and airing of ideas over Twitter, Facebook and blogs tends to dilute or mitigate against unorthodox viewpoints.

The result is that there is little incentive for radical expression or thinking ... It feels that the whole news agenda is written to a giant algorithm, where people's energies are spent disparaging each other rather than saying anything constructive or meaningful. The geeks have inherited the earth and, to date at least, no-one seems to have found what will replace this new opiate of the masses.'

I found all this deeply depressing. I don't want to live in a world like this.

I like radicalism.

I like outrage.

10.3. HUMANITY CAN OVERCOME TECHNOLOGY

I want people to stand up and be counted.

I'm not arguing against these brainy guys (who, at my school, we would have called geeks). Indeed, I fear they might be right. But are they? Is there a ray of hope? Can we overcome these geeks?

I think we can. It is called humanity.

In these fragmented times, where we have more connectivity, but more divergence, than ever before, it is harder than ever to stand out from the crowd; to break through the media morass; to lead, with conviction and with integrity, and change the world.

Winston Churchill, Martin Luther King and JFK did it. Nelson Mandela has done it. Yes, even The Iron Lady inspired change through the sheer force of her conviction and personality.

And, in this year of a Presidential Election in the United States, especially for those of us who witnessed his address (and great opening gag!) to the UK Parliament on 25 May last year, it is hard to imagine a world where Barack Obama will not be re-elected.

Over here, none of our leaders can touch Obama for the way he himself touches people. His charm, charisma and style are based on unimpeachable principles of honesty and moral integrity that not one of our lot can sniff at, let alone claim. America, be proud.

Whatever your politics, however much of a geek you are, you have to have faith that human beings can rise above technology and touch people with meaning and with soul.

For, if not, what is there to live for?

10.4. Digital Fish Fight Drives Democracy

17 March 2014 09:06

For several years now, I have advocated that more intelligent use of the media options available to us in the 21st century can influence social change and a better world.

Earlier this month, we were reminded of such a campaign when TV chef Hugh Fearnley-Whittingstall updated TV viewers on his 'Fish Fight' campaign.

For those who are not aware, Fish Fight started in 2010 when F-W highlighted the ridiculous situation where, under the EU landing quota system, our fishermen were being forced to throw back into the sea over half of the dead fish they had caught.

Largely as a result of the Fish Fight campaign, there was an emphatic vote in the European parliament in which MEPs voted 502 to 137 to end this ridiculous practice. Fish Fight has been, in every sense, a political campaign.

Here's what you should bear in mind should you fish to fight such a cause yourself:

The audacity of simplicity.

The less arguable your cause, the more effective will be your campaign. Let's face it, Fish Fight is a no-brainer. Would any sane person, or should I say non-politician, not agree that once you have caught some dead fish, there's no point chucking them back into the sea? No less than 870 million people go hungry in this world. These fish need eating.

Identify your target.

If you are seeking social change, at some point or another you have to engage with politicians and/or civil servants. In my experience, people who work in the public sector are slippery. You have to pin them down. Put them in plaice.

10.4. DIGITAL FISH FIGHT DRIVES DEMOCRACY

A human being (not a job title).

Make sure your target is a living, breathing human being – and identifiable as such. There's no point baiting an abominable no-man. You need someone who has the power to say yes – and, ideally, someone who has something to lose. Fish Fight's target was the EU fisheries commissioner, Maria Damanaki. You may not have heard of her, but let me tell you she has heard of Hugh's Fish Fight!

Cause celeb.

Celebs are very important in society today. They do not have to be high achievers or, for that matter, to do or have done anything at all: no intelligence; no insight; no industry; not even good behaviour. They don't even have to be pretty (although it helps). Fish Fight landed Stephen Fry, Ricky Gervais, Jamie Oliver and Jeremy Paxman. If the skipper of your campaign, the captain of the ship, is a celeb like Hugh so much the better.

Rent a quote.

Celebs know how to make news. Jeremy Paxman said this about Fish Fight: 'If this policy is conservation, I'm the Mad Hatter'. Sensible people don't care whether Mr Paxman sees himself as the Mad Hatter or not. Luckily, for you, the media do. Celebs make news.

Play the media.

The media aren't interested in the merits of your case. But they do write and talk about celebs. Large sections of the media don't do anything else. Play them at their own game. Feed them titbits. Make them bite. Reel them in.

Don't pay the media.

Unlike consumer products or price comparison websites, you haven't got the money to buy the media space you need to present your case. You are a sprat, not a mackerel.

TV.

TV is vital. Whatever people tell you about 'digital', television is the most powerful media channel there is. But TV is expensive. So you need to persuade your celebrities to persuade a production company to persuade a commissioning editor to persuade a TV channel to broadcast a documentary about your cause. Fish Fight has been watched by over 3million in the UK and repeated in 28 countries worldwide. Hugh knows the TV game. He is a celeb.

Digital.
Now we're talking! Fish Fight has attracted 258,777 Facebook likes; 51,052 followers on Twitter; 349,688 views on YouTube; 12million page views on the web page. Whatever your 'digital' agency might tell you, these numbers alone are not enough. Oh no, they're not. You have to activate these people – get them to do something.

Activate your followers.
870,000 Fish Fighters from 195 countries signed the petition. 174,000 sent emails to Ms Damanaki and other MEPs. German Fish Fighters sent 29,400 emails to MEP Werner Kuhn. Blimey, that's more than I get after each post on this blog. 'When people take action, politicians have to listen', says Hugh.

Retail pressure.
Second only to celebs, the media love news about supermarkets. If you can get your supporters to boycott products or, preferably, whole chains of supermarkets your campaign is in the basket. Hugh says supermarket is backtracking on its public pledge to sell sustainable fish. 'Top chef accuses Tesco: If you care about our oceans, take this tuna off your shelves'.

Summary.
'A dumb European law has actually been changed, by a British TV chef and the hundreds of thousands who got behind his Fish Fight campaign. That's bloody brilliant, moving even.'
So there you go. That's how Fish Fight hit the back of the net.
That's enough of this.
I need a drink…

10.5. Mourning Big Brother and exposure of social prejudice

19 September 2010 22:05

The late Big Brother exposed a good deal of media and cultural snobbery.

Last week, a BBC Radio5Live presenter was unbelievably patronising to his listeners who called to support Big Brother (and the 3.7million who watched the last show).

I am not ashamed to admit that I believe Big Brother played a vitally important social role in exposing underlying prejudice in society.

Indeed, I would go so far as to say that, through the years, Big Brother not only entertained me and my children, but it enabled us to address subjects that we may not otherwise have discussed.

I am not referring to Celebrity Big Brother here. I am talking about the show that featured 'normal' people.

Mind you, by winning the celebrity show as a mere 'normal' person in 2006, Chantelle Houghton (I admit to relying on Wikipedia here), famously exposed the celebrities as the shallow, sub-normal people most of them really are.

So why was the 'normal' Big Brother both entertaining and socially important?

And why do I believe that the world Big Brother exposed was important not only to my children and me, but also to all of us whose livelihoods depend on understanding and influencing human behaviour?

Well, frankly, and this is an interesting social observation in itself, each series of Big Brother inevitably included at least one person who we would not normally meet, either in the course of our day-to-day personal lives or in the focus groups on which we depend so much (or, should I say, 'we depend too much'?)

Typically, these people do not fall into the demographic profiles of those whose behaviour we seek to influence. They are off of our radar, off the wall and, often, off their heads. They are different – from us and from each other. That's what makes them so interesting.

Call me clossetted, but until I 'met' Pete Bennett on Big Brother, also in 2006, I had never met anyone with Tourette's Syndrome. But I'm glad I got to know him and was delighted he won the show.

Call me naïve, but I had never come across a Portuguese transsexual like Nadia Almada who, on the recent 'Ultimate Big Brother', attracted transphobic comments from another contestant for which he was removed from the show.

Call me illiterate, but I'm not sure I would have known what the word 'transphobic' meant until I researched this post so diligently.

Call me a snob, but most of my personal friends and professional contacts know there was a bloke called William Shakespeare, they don't think East Anglia is abroad and it probably wouldn't cross their minds to say: "Posh and Becks named their baby Brooklyn because he was conceived there. What am I going to call my baby? Jacuzzi?"

There are lots of other examples. Google them, Bing them, Wiki them, whatever.

My serious point is this.

Almost without exception, the Big Brother contestants, when their true nature was revealed during the course of the show, were different from the way my kids and I perceived them when they first entered the house.

This is a very important lesson for us all. When we meet people, we label them, we make instant judgements and it takes time to discover what they are really like.

It is like this in marketing and communications.

We can develop all the consumer research, test marketing, strategic thinking and creative brilliance in the world, but we never know for sure how people are going to behave.

And it is always worth bearing this in mind.

Thank you Big Brother.

10.6. THE PERVERSE CULT OF CELEBRITY

16 October 2012 09:01

When I was at school, we had a visiting preacher in Chapel who told us there were three things in his sermon that we would never forget. And I haven't. They were:

Don't poison Socrates.

Don't crucify Christ.

Stand up and be counted.

At times in my life, I have thought of these three mantras, particularly the last one in which I have my own little track record.

I have thought about it while watching and listening to pious celebrities pontificating about the perverted behaviour of that famous celebrity Jimmy Savile.

Not only was Jimmy Savile a celebrity, he was a BBC celebrity.

Once, at a Ball at an expensively famous London hotel, the seating plan had me sitting next to a BBC celebrity. I had never seen or heard of her. Apparently she read the news.

When it came to sit down, this famous person I had never heard of moved her place up one so her husband was sitting next to me. Next to her, another famous BBC news reader I had never heard of did the same thing which meant they sat next to each other flanked, guarded, by their husbands, one of whom told me they always do this. It protects them from 'the public' (like me).

Who on earth do these people think they are?

Apparently a lot of them heard about what Jimmy Savile was up to. Some of them say they *knew* what he was up to. But none of them did anything about it. 'It wouldn't have been worth it', they say. 'No one would have done anything.'

Shouldn't they have reported it anyway?

As it happens, I do not believe they did not report him because they thought no one would do anything. I think they kept quiet because they see themselves as 'celebrities'. And there is an 'honour amongst thieves' rule among celebrities that they don't tread on each others turf. They don't have to behave in the same way as lesser mortals like us.

I admit, occasionally, a celebrity will slag off another celebrity. When they do, it makes headlines. When you think about it, it is surprising how little it does happen, given the way they behave.

And who are they, these 'celebrities'?

Some people segment them into 'A Listers' and 'B Listers'. The A Listers have a rare and wonderful talent like great actors or musicians or writers or record-breaking Olympic athletes (who, ironically, do not feel too superior to engage with the plebs in the crowd).

The B Listers are what you might call 'media' celebrities. These people are talentless nonentities who, in my view, have done nothing at all to warrant the 'celebrity' title. They either have a famous mummy or daddy or they do something which millions of other people could do too such as appear on reality shows or they read the news (couldn't a monkey be trained to do this?)

In this context, Jimmy Savile – Sir Jimmy Savile no less – was surely a B Lister. Apparently not. It emerges that people at the BBC and other media channels worshipped the ground he walked on to the extent that he was above the law.

Really?

A bloke who, on TV, looks at an autocue and says 'Now for the gorgeous Pan's People' followed by some inane donkey-like noise and a cloud of cigar-smoke? The guy who, on radio, puts a record on a turntable and tells you the name of the band? Or who tells his next victim that he will 'Fix It' for something to happen while his hand gently, creepily caresses its way up and down the poor child's back?

This guy – this pervert – was above the law.

Who says he was above the law?

Well these other 'celebrities' do. With their 'celebrity' attitude and behaviour towards each other, they were part of the cover up. They did not report him.

Why didn't these B List people 'stand up and be counted'?

Didn't they think of the poor under-aged children who were the victims?

10.7. THE PERVERSE CULT OF CELEBRITY

Where do these celebrities put their morality, their human conscience, their social responsibility?

It is up their own backsides, that's where it is. And there is nothing I would like more than for someone to find evidence on these self-serving, gutless 'celebrities' and have them locked up for perverting the course of justice.

That's what I said:

Perverting the course of justice.

11

RANDOM CONSUMER INSIGHTS

11.1. A Breath of Fresh Air for Health Clubs and Gyms

5 November 2010 08:08

It is a truth universally acknowledged that getting dressed is best on a dry floor.

This applies more to health clubs and gyms than it would in your home. I know this because I undertook a quantitative research study to confirm this important market dynamic. My only respondent was my wife – but I know from experience that if we agree then that is enough evidence to confirm the truth of any subject.

In any case, as anyone in marketing and communications knows, statistics exist to be manipulated to one's advantage.

For example, I claim to visit my gym three times a week. I go once mid-week and once at week-ends but if the weekday visits are on say, Wednesdays, then that adds up to three visits in eight days, which is not much more than a week, is it?

That's the story I tell my doctor and I'm sticking to it. Such is the nature of statistics.

Anyway, I am seeking to overcome the following dilemma in health clubs and gyms.

On leaving the shower, it is impossible to dry one's feet. Yes, one can attempt to do so having exited one's shower but then walking the aisle back to the changing room only makes them wet again – for the showers are still furiously spewing out water after one has left them because they only turn off on an automatic basis.

This means, inevitably, that the floors of the changing rooms get wet because one has to walk through the shower area to get back into the changing room.

So, having returned to the wet-floored changing room to get dressed, one is required to put Foot One into one's sock and then balance, and perhaps even hop about, on Foot Two so that Foot One (with the sock) can dangle in the air to avoid touching the wet floor before putting it into Foot One's shoe. Please believe me when I say that one can feel slightly ridiculous performing this ungracious, arrhythmic dance.

The alternative is disaster. For nothing can be quite so uncomfortable than slipping a wet sock into a dry shoe. Or you could even slip over altogether. Health and safety!

Now, I think I have a radically innovative solution to this important problem.

In my health club — and further extensive research has shown that mine is not the only health club to carry this feature — there is a hand drier in the lavatorial area. You know, one of those machines that blows out hot air when you put your hands beneath them. Recently, I have read that these hand drying machines spread more bugs than not using them at all. I hope this does not apply to the showers that appear to carry the same auto on-off technology.

So what is my solution?

Well, surely the automatic hand dryer machines are wasted in their current position?

After all, one picks up one's own towel as one enters the changing room. A towel is essential to the gymming and swimming process.

Why do you need hand dryers in the lavatorial areas?

Wouldn't these machines, rather than be fixed four feet from the floor in the lavatories, be better placed one foot from the floor on the exit from the showers?

This way, one could blow-dry one's feet under said machines, and perhaps even perform a dainty little samba, before entering the beautifully dry changing-room to get dressed without having to overcome the hateful wet-sock-dry-shoe syndrome?

I appreciate, especially on Guy Fawkes Day, that this little Insight won't set the world on fire.

But it might provide just a few people with a small degree of comfort.

11.2. Retail search (not)

27 November 2009 17:01

Recently, my family and I have had major, multiple retail problems. Personally, a fundamental shift has been forced onto my purchasing behaviour. My local Somerfield has become a Co-op.

On the good side, the place looks cleaner in every way, they sent me a discount voucher booklet which was handy because I like discounts – they even offered me a discount for my funeral.

And, most important to me, the Co-op retained the staff from Somerfield – all of whom I like. They have always been nice, polite people and I admire them a lot. They work hard and they smile at me and say 'good morning' or 'good evening' and 'thank you' when I buy things from them.

A few years ago, Somerfield tried to replace these kind, helpful staff with machines where you scanned in your own goods and then paid for them automatically. But I made a stand. I refused to use these machines. They didn't smile at me and they didn't say 'good morning' and 'thank you'. The check-out people were right behind me and, quite quickly, we repelled these horrible, faceless, mutant machines. I refused to use them and the check-out staff continued to be unfailingly polite to me.

Power to the people!

So, I like the Co-op and I hope their new store works for them. But I do have a problem with them, and it is a problem which might actually be a problem for the Co-op more than me. I'll come back to that.

In the meantime, having said I like the people at the Co-op, at least I find it easy to approach them when they move the stock around the shelves – which I am told is a tactic retailers use to promote impulse purchasing by their regular customers.

But moving on, as it were, last week my wife had a whole new problem. Here's the story:

THOUGHTS ON LIFE AND ADVERTISING

We went to buy a sofa on Sunday. And we had invited some friends round to our house for a drink that evening. No big deal. Just one other couple and their daughter who is a friend of our daughter. We had some wine and even some gin in stock but we had run out of tonic and we needed some juice for our sweet girls and some snacks and some dips. I'm a guacamole man myself (unlike Peter Mandelson who likes mushy peas, I'm told).

The plan was we would buy the sofa and then we would go to Asda, where my wife does her weekly Monday-morning shop, for the nibbles.

But things don't always go to plan and, in this case, we took much longer than we thought we would not buying a sofa. We found what we wanted. But twelve weeks delivery? What's all that about? We want one now!

Anyway, near the sofa shop there was a Tesco. Great, we thought, let's see how the real people live in the big, wide world. We'll pop in there. So we did. We bought all the drinks and nibbles we needed. It was a bit crowded, but it seemed a great place – lots of offers, lots of different things and even an upstairs bit and a petrol forecourt outside.

So impressed was my wife that she announced that, the next day, she would do her Monday-morning shop at Tesco instead of Asda.

In the event, she had a nightmare. She had her standard list of things to buy but she couldn't find anything! Up and down the aisles she went. She found this at that end of the store, that at the other end of the store and went off her trolley pushing it up aisle and down aisle.

Sure, there are signs above the aisles but lime pickle? What is it? A 'sauce'? An 'international food'? Or is it a 'dip' like those we had bought the day before? No one seemed to know. And the whole process took three hours – twice as long as Asda.

Which brings me back to my Co-op problem. I can't find anything!

Remember, I like my new Co-op, I like the people who work there and I like that Co-op kept their jobs for them. But when it was a Somerfield, I knew where everything was and I popped in there most days to buy a little bit of this and a little bit of that.

Now I don't bother. I'm in a pickle. And that's why I think the Co-op are in a pickle too. Quite simply, I am not spending as much there as I did when it was a Somerfield. And my wife never wants to go to Tesco again.

She's sticking with Asda, thanks.

11.2. RETAIL SEARCH (NOT)

So, isn't it strange that for all this world of 'search' that we live in, and for all the millions they spend urging us to go to this one instead of that one – including, no doubt, how to search for them online – these major multiples can't find a better way of telling us where anything is when we go to their stores?

11.3. Privacy in-store and out

22 February 2010 23:02

So, from Gordon Brown to Tiger Woods, Ashley Cole to John Terry, all has been revealed. There's nothing we don't know.

In the personal lives of these great men, the girls – and I am afraid there have been lots of them – have been only bit-part players. Even the mini-skirted 'Brown Sugars' have been outed to an insatiable electorate.

For me, apart from sympathy for their other halves, I don't really care what these people get up to in private. I wouldn't expect anything else from the footballers and I even have a tinge of sympathy for Tiger Woods.

As for Gordon Brown at University, I would be more interested in comparing his political philosophy at the time to the thriving market economy he manages now. I can't stand career politicians. Get a life!

And then, a couple of days ago, The Sunday Times (online) wrote:

"Gordon Brown's rebranding efforts continued apace today with another emotional interview focusing on…the death of his mother".

This came "ahead of the Tesco magazine Mum of the Year awards". There must be lessons here for Brand Republicans:

Gordon Brown – branding – personal information – Tesco

My other hat links all this to an everyday shopping experience that I absolutely detest. It makes me cringe, look the other way and sometimes even walk out of the store.

I am talking about pharmacists like Boots and Superdrug as well as major multiples like Tesco.

How undignified is it to shop in these places?

Do I really want to know that it is the time of the month for the lady in front? Or that the guy ahead of her is planning a big night out with his condoms and KY? Or that the guy behind me has a haemorrhoid problem?

11.3. PRIVACY IN-STORE AND OUT

When those Martians come down to Earth one day and discover we eat potatos not powder, won't they laugh at us humans revealing such personal information to complete strangers (or worse, sometimes, to people we know) by forcing us to carry personal items in open baskets?

Can't these stores persuade some bung-ho pharmaceutical companies to sponsor and brand opaque shopping baskets with 'privacy flaps'?

Or, perhaps, give us eco-friendly, re-cycled paper bags to put in our baskets so we can keep our personal products private?

Can't their check-outs be more discreetly designed?

And staff trained accordingly?

To those of us who aren't 'celebs' and don't matter at all, the great unwashed as it were, why do we put up with such personal indignity?

From Gordon Brown down, what an uncivilised society we are.

11.4. Halfords Bicycle Chase

16 May 2011 08:16

It had been agreed that the wife needed a new bicycle. As the old one had expired, ceased to be and gone to meet its maker this was indeed a 'need' and not a 'want'.

I had just sat down in my comfy armchair with a lovely Saturday morning cuppa and was about to read the newspaper, a pleasure that some people of my generation still enjoy, and in she walked:

"I'm off to Halfords to buy a new bicycle".

"What, just like that?" I said.

"Well, we agreed I need one", she replied.

"Yes, I know darling. But you don't wander off to a shop and buy one. Not anymore. You look around online. You check for second-hand bargains, see what's on offer. You compare prices. It's a whole different meerkat these days".

She's used to my witty repartee.

So we set off on the campaign trail. She's tall and needs a 21" frame. That's the brief.

She hits the PC upstairs. I browse the phone downstairs, happy in my armchair.

First, because I'm that kinda guy, I check the second-hand options (Manchester and Leicester – not convenient for Battersea). Then I search for local bicycle shops. They might be cheaper. I call a couple. Nothing doing.

Finally, the inevitable happens. I hit the Halfords website and – lo and behold! – there is just the bike she needs. The 21" frame Apollo Highway Trekking Hybrid Bike. And, what's more, reduced from £359.99 to 179.99.

We're off to the races!

The wife agrees this looks a perfect choice and, with her slightest 'I told you so' sigh, announces she is heading off to Halfords as she was going to do over an hour earlier.

11.4. HALFORDS BICYCLE CHASE

Feeling humbled, I offer to come with her. If the bike is right, she can ride it back and I'll drive the car home. Halfords is only a mile away, their website informs me. In fact, their website says 'we go the extra mile' but, in our case, they did not need to.

Into Halfords we saunter, happy Saturday shoppers. Oh look – there's a tent!

That might be useful for our daughter. And a lilo (aka 'airbed mattress')! Could be good for the summer holiday. And some other bits and pieces that may come in useful.

Then we go upstairs to the bicycle department. And there, all resplendent, is the Apollo Highway Trekking Hybrid Bike – but only the 18" frame model.

"Don't worry" says the very useful and friendly assistant *"we've got six 21" frames out the back. I am sure that'll fit you just grand. It'll be ready tomorrow".*

At this stage, I feel I have to intervene:

"It says here the price is £219.99. I'm sure the website said £179.99. Are you sure this is the same bike?"

"Oh yes, sir, that's the 'online' price. This is the 'in store' price".

"So if I go back home and order the same bike online, it'll be £40 less?"

"Yes."

"Do you deliver it or do we come back to pick it up?"

"You can come back and pick it up, sir. Like I say, it'll be ready tomorrow."

"But I've got my phone on me. Can I go online here and order it now for £40 less than the price it says on this tag on the bicycle in front of me?"

"Of course, sir. The order will come up on my till in a couple of minutes."

So that is what we did. The next day, we picked it up (for £179.99).

The moral of the story is that if you want to buy a new bicycle from Halfords, don't go to their rather large store (for which they must pay a rather large rent), don't be surprised that their range of products is wider than you had thought and certainly don't be tempted into buying anything else.

It's not worth it.

Just find what you want on their website, see if it is in stock (the website will tell you this), cruise down to the shop to check the bike fits ok and then go home and buy it.

Or do what I did and take your phone and pay the cheaper 'online price' while you are standing in the store.

Huh?

11.5. Marks & Spencer – A Customer Insight

12 November 2010 08:19

This week Marc Bolland, the new CEO of M&S, unveiled his strategic plan, including a target to grow internet sales from £500m now to between £800m and £1bn in 2014.

I'm sure you can Google the rest.

One analyst described the review as 'sensible but a little underwhelming'. Apparently the strategy is to 'keep doing what M&S does – only better'.

Well I can tell you that, from a consumer perspective, this won't be good enough.

I am qualified to say this because I have shopped in our local M&S for over 20 years. Indeed, with Paxman-like effrontery, I can reveal that I have never bought a pair of underpants from anywhere else.

And here is the problem facing the M&S brand:

Cheap clothes. Expensive food.

I exaggerate to make my point but it is like merging Primark with Harrods Food Hall.

The two just don't go together.

With so many High Street stores from which, for car parking reasons, customers are unable to load their trolleys and fill their boots, there is a limit to the amount of food that can be physically carried from most M&S stores. So I do understand they have to make a bigger margin on their bespoke, up-market food offering.

But then, having treated themselves to these fancy (but pricey) delicacies, M&S customers have to walk out past ranges of clothing that are cheap as chips.

This is the strategic dilemma facing M&S. As he is on a £15m pay package, I suspect Marc Bolland is more caviar than pants and will work this one out.

He needs to.

11.6. WHAT'S IN A NAME?

12 April 2010 23:19

When does a name become a brand? And at what stage of a brand's development can it rely on the mere transmission of its name to justify expenditure on the exposure of its name alone?

For example, how do marketers justify investment in the presence of their name on the side of a golf ball, or the side-line of a football pitch or the side-pod of the nose-cone of a Formula One car?

I have never really understood this side of our market. These 'sponsorship' brands aren't making a claim. They rely on their name.

To people who do not understand the meaning of the word 'brand', I advise them to substitute the word 'brand' with the word 'personality'.

Once they have understood this, they can then understand that brands rely very heavily on their name. In fact, for most brands, their name defines the brand, although there are some exceptions, such as Nike and Shell, where a visual device says it all. These are formula one brands.

There is an inherent truth behind these brand names. People know what they stand for and what they can get out of them.

Thus, I suppose, 'reminding' people of a brand name alone is money well spent. Personally, I still don't get it, but people do it – so it must be justifiable expenditure.

In the real world, having established a brand like say, Dove, the brand's personality can be extended into new product areas and new income streams. But you need to connect the claim of old brand to delivery in new product.

And in the High Street, signage is very important. The name of the store, even if it is as fatuous as Fat Face, defines the personality of the brand and so encourages shoppers to feel comfortable entering the store.

Unfortunately, these days, it seems the same shops with the same signs and the same personalities are all on the same-looking High Streets in same-looking towns. Wherever you go, the names are the same.

Talking of towns, I have always been interested in the fact that people have a preconceived perception about a place that may not be based on reality, and where they may never have even been. For example, why has Slough always been defined as such a rotten borough? It can't all be down to one poem by John Betjeman.

Indeed, the place I live and work also seems to be looked down on by certain folk, especially those North of the River Thames.

Why is that the case and how can one change it?

When I moved The Salmon Agency to Clapham Junction 10 years ago, we were paying £12 per square foot compared to over £50 a square foot in Victoria – 7 minutes away on a train.

Because Clapham Junction is a 'main line' rather than a 'tube' station, people think you have to wait for a train or find a timetable – unlike the Underground, where you just turn up hoping a train will turn up too.

Unless you live near Clapham Junction, that is, in which case you will know that trains to Victoria and Waterloo leave every few minutes.

In fact, in terms of frequency of trains to London, to all intents and purposes, Clapham Junction operates as an Underground station – one stop to Vauxhall, two stops to Waterloo and, often, one stop to Victoria.

You seldom have to wait more than five minutes for a train into town.

So I have always told visitors to my office that Clapham Junction raises an interesting branding issue based on people's automatic perceptions of a 'main line' rather than 'tube' station.

But Clapham Junction has another, much bigger branding issue.

Clapham Junction is not in Clapham at all. It is in Battersea.

Clapham is the other side of Clapham Common and Wandsworth is the other side of Wandsworth Common and Clapham Junction is bang between the two – in Battersea.

That brand 'Clapham Junction' is not based on an inherent truth. It is where it isn't.

And it is really boring when you live and work here and tourists come out of the station, often laden with baggage from Gatwick, and ask the directions for a road in Clapham and you have to tell them they are not in Clapham at all.

It doesn't give visitors a favourable first impression of London.

I also think it is really important for the people who live here to have a positive sense of identity about the area they live in.

11.6. WHAT'S IN A NAME?

So I wonder if towns and urban areas like Clapham Junction could identify and admit to their inherent truth (or lack of).

Would Clapham Junction benefit from a change of name to, say, Battersea Junction and could marketing and communications experts use this to launch and establish a greater sense of pride and identity in a place just like they do with 'brands'?

And, if this could be done, could the new name signal a new direction and a new sense of identity and a new sense of pride and maybe even better behaviour and respect for people within their neighbourhood?

I wish.

11.7. Galaxy Chocolate Makes the Book World Sick

19 November 2010 08:30

Now, from the start, I have to own up to two vested interests.

First, I am a plain chocolate, not a milk chocolate person. Give me Bournville over Dairy Milk any day – or, preferably, Co-op Fairtrade dark chocolate. Yummy.

Second, I am the founder of Lovereading.co.uk.

So I know about the Book Trade. And I know the book trade is in a bad way. Waterstone's are the only book chain on the High Street, until they unite with HMV. I don't count WH Smith, other than their airport stores, which aren't on High Streets. By definition, they are at ground level. Boom, boom.

And I know about the effect of the end of the Net Book Agreement in 1995, which has enabled major multiples to sell bestselling books at substantial discounts – sometimes, ridiculously, such as with the last Harry Potter, at a loss.

And I know this has polarised the book market between the bestsellers and the rest, which is why literary giants like Katie Price and Gordon Ramsay dominate the charts.

And I know that virtually every book that has ever been published is available on the internet – which is fine if you know what you want to buy, but not great if you would like some help and guidance on which book you might enjoy reading next (hence lovereading.co.uk).

And I know that many of the friendly, local independent bookstores – those owned by human beings who love books and know books and know you and know which books you might like to read – have struggled to survive. Or haven't.

And I know all this makes it really difficult for new authors' books to break through.

11.7. GALAXY CHOCOLATE MAKES THE BOOK WORLD SICK

Because of technology, it is easier than ever to get your book printed and published – you can do it yourself through print-on-demand (POD). But, paradoxically, it has become harder than ever to enable readers to discover it. You can stick it online, but you almost certainly won't find a bricks and mortar bookstore to stock it.

Here are two Insights that are unique to the book market and very important.

Unlike any other market I have worked in, in the book market, it is the new books that are discounted. Thanks to the collapse of the Net Book Agreement, you can buy all the latest bestsellers at half-price (or less). If you want to buy a book that was published some time ago, although it is new to you, it either won't be available at all (in a supermarket) or you will have to find it at the back of Waterstone's racked, illogically, in alphabetical order by name of author, at the back of the store – or they will order it for you. And the 'old' book will be available at full price.

In this case, you might as well go home or back to the office and buy it online at a discount – but still not as great a discount as the new books on offer.

This is mad but true. Would a supermarket sell you fresh lettuce at a discount and charge more for last week's stock? Of course not. It would be commercial suicide. But this is what happens in the Book Trade.

The other Insight is that, in books, you don't know what you are buying. The pages you are paying to read, that you hope will fire your imagination, entrance you with someone else's thoughts and take you into another world will, by definition, be new.

Other products like, say, Marmite or Corn Flakes, provide guaranteed taste and texture. You know what you are going to get. I once sat on a pavement in Saigon with an executive from Heineken, pouring bottle after bottle of past-sell-by-date beer into the gutter. Such was his commitment into the consistency of taste and integrity of his product that he had even bought and paid retail price for this redundant stock.

So, with a book, you need guidance and reassurance, before you start reading it. Before you buy it, you want to know that it is going to be good.

This was the dynamic behind the amazing success of the Richard & Judy Book Club. Why them? No idea. But it shows how desperate readers are for guidance.

Another way of reassuring readers that a book is worth reading is if it has been nominated for, or won, a book award. Because people do read.

Millions of them. They just want the comfort of knowing they will enjoy the book they have chosen.

So I approve of Book Awards. And, as I live and work within the dynamics of a market economy, I understand that Book Awards need sponsorship.

One such Book Award is sponsored by Galaxy chocolate.

'As sponsor of the Awards, Galaxy continues to unite reading and chocolate as the perfect match for women everywhere to enjoy their ultimate me time moment', gushed 'Galaxy Ambassador' Claudia Winkleman at the Awards Ceremony.

Why just 'women'? Why 'ambassador'?

Why?

Sponsorship is one thing, but now things get really sticky.

Personally speaking, I find the connection between chocolate and books contrived and rather tasteless, but if Galaxy advertising claims 'melting into a good book with some silky smooth Galaxy chocolate is a wonderful indulgence', what do I know?

What I really object to is the next line of the advertising and the next stage of the process, the sales promotion – 'Galaxy are giving away a million books'.

Yes, you read that correctly – giving away and a million. Not 'up to a million'. Not even 'over a million'. A clearly and specifically defined statement of fact. A promise. Galaxy are giving away free, not a hundred, not a thousand, not a hundred thousand but a million books. Who on earth conceived and approved this counter-effective and, I hope, sales-counter-reductive idea?

What effect is it going to have on the struggling Book Trade?

What threat will it be to the endangered independent bookstores in lost sales?

How many of these books would otherwise have been bought by readers?

And, if not these books, what other books might these readers have chosen?

Or will these books be given away as cheap Christmas presents?

Or be found, for years to come, un-read in charity shops up and down the country?

What 'value' is this going to add to the perception of books in general?

I am afraid I cannot answer these questions, which is why I am asking them, but I have diligently undertaken some market research and bought

11.7. GALAXY CHOCOLATE MAKES THE BOOK WORLD SICK

four bars of Galaxy. Even though I can't stand the stuff, I melted into action.

What you do is go to their website and enter an 'indulgent code' provided by Galaxy. My indulgent codes were 'poetry', 'dream', 'virtue' and 'subtle'. You then enter ten random letters (which is quite tedious, particularly as they are not very legible). And then you are told you haven't won.

But the wrapper says that 'if you are a winner, you can indicate your top two preferences from a list of books, one of which you should receive'.

And the website says the choices are 'Her Fearful Symmetry' by Audrey Niffenegger, 'Wedding Season' by Katie Fforde, 'The Truth about Melody Browne' by Lisa Jewell, 'The Beach House' by Jane Green and 'Knots & Crosses' by Ian Rankin. All books by successful authors and all with convenient links to their own websites.

I would say, to give them their due, that Galaxy is not using this as a data collection exercise other than to 'Like' their Facebook page (as, at the time of writing, 594,335 sad people have done). Apparently this gives you another chance to win a free book.

Anyway, having bought my four bars of sickly Galaxy chocolate, and read the packaging, I can tell you that this rather tasteless promotion ends on 25 May 2011.

We can then take a view on how much this little gimmick has cost the Book Trade and, in particular, the independent bookstores who are struggling so hard to survive.

And all for a few bars of 'sugar, cocoa ingredients (cocoa butter, mass), skimmed milk powder, milk fat, whey powder, vegetable fat, emulsifier (soya lecithin), natural vanilla extract. Milk chocolate contains milk solids 14% minimum and cocoa solids 25% maximum plus vegetable fats in addition to cocoa butter'.

For these are the ingredients required to 'melt' into a good book.

12

DO AS YOU WOULD BE DONE BY

12.1. KINDNESS? THAT TAKES EFFORT

28 DECEMBER 2012 08:58

This post on kindness was going to be my Christmas message until the massacre in Newtown forced me, and many others, to rage against the inhumanity of the US gun laws.

Mind you, even at Sandy Hook, there was evidence of extraordinary human behaviour: 'What we forget, too often, is the kindness and resilience of this nation.' And, way beyond kindness, who will forget the heroic bravery of Victoria Soto and her colleagues?

On 18 November, the TV producer John Lloyd was on Desert Island Discs. He is behind such programmes as Spitting Image, Not The Nine o'Clock News, QI and, yippee, Blackadder. In a surprisingly introspective interview, this cultured and educated man said:

'Intelligence is something you're given. Kindness? That takes effort.'

It emerged that Lloyd has developed a personal philosophy based, largely, on what he felt to have been unfair and cruel treatment by people he thought were friends and on 'The Book: On the Taboo Against Being Who You Are', written by the mystical Alan Watts in 1966.

Through personal experience, I have seen there is a nice way to do something – or a nasty way. This is a choice. For example, dismissing someone from their job is always going to distress the person concerned, but how many companies and executives ask themselves 'We need to do this nasty thing, so how can we do it kindly?' It doesn't happen, does it?

As John Lloyd said: 'Kindness? That takes effort.'

Making the effort to be kind is nothing new. In 'Rhetoric', Aristotle defined kindness as: 'helpfulness towards someone in need, not in return for anything, nor for the advantage of the helper himself, but for that of the person helped'.

As such, isn't kindness something we should have more of?

Mind you, as I have found to my cost (20p in fact), kindness can rebound.

You all know about Sachin, my local newsagent. One day, I was in his shop and, as I was chatting to him, a young boy came in and browsed the comics on display. He selected one and said to Sachin:

'How much is this, please?'

'99p'

'I've only got 80p' said the boy, lips quivering, eyes watering.

So crestfallen was the child that, kind-hearted and generous as ever, I took some loose change out of my pocket and gave him a 20p coin.

'There you are. You can buy that comic now' I said, saintly.

At this point, the boy grabbed the coin from my hand and comic-less, but 20p richer, ran out of the shop.

I looked up at Sachin as he shook his head and rolled his eyes:

'You're so naïve, Hugh' he said, wisely.

I think my interest in kindness came from my father. Many of my generation, whose fathers fought in the Second World War, are conscious of how kind their fathers were. Perhaps, by experiencing the horrors of war, they evolved a philosophy of kindness which, these days, many of us will not have thought of – let alone adopt as a conscious standard of behaviour.

For myself, I had my own experience of man's inhumanity to man on an early visit to the War Museum in Saigon which I described in post 5.5. How can one forget such horrors in one's day-to-day life, especially when experienced first hand? Perhaps we should find ways to pay for our underclasses to visit such places.

On 14 November, a few days before John Lloyd was on Desert Island Discs in England, was the story of Larry DePrimo, a police officer in New York who took pity on a homeless person and made the effort to go to a shoe shop and buy the vagrant some new boots.

This 'simple act of kindness (has) become a worldwide inspiration' and, as an example of the goodness of social media, went viral on Facebook.

In the face of the horror of Sandy Hook, perhaps now would be a good time to celebrate the kindness of the American people and hope that this basic human instinct will prevail.

And perhaps one might consider for what kind intention has a good guy a gun?

Happy New Year.

12.2. Crossing the road

8 March 2010 22:49

So, David Cameron and Michael Gove want us to adopt the Swedish education model.

I once had an educational, indeed enlightening, experience in Sweden.

It involved a media channel that may never be used for commercial purposes – but which is very important. In fact, it can save lives.

I am talking about the little red and green 'men' that light up on and off at pedestrian crossings. Their aim is to tell you whether or not it is safe to cross the road. (Can I call them 'men'? Probably not, especially in Sweden. But I'm not there now.)

Anyway, there I was in a provincial Swedish town, with my better half, clutching the hands of our two toddler children and waiting to cross a road – as it happened, a very straight road.

And we waited. And waited.

Some people joined us. And then some more.

The red 'man' was alight. He stayed alight. And he stayed alight.

He just wasn't moving.

In fact, nothing was moving.

I looked left. No traffic for miles.

I looked right. No traffic for miles.

I looked left again. And right again. And left again.

"Why don't these other people cross the road", I asked my better half.

"Because we are with children", she said. "Otherwise they would".

Would the Conservatives, or any other of our revered career-politicians, succeed in educating our children to behave in such a thoughtful and civilised way when they grow up?

12.3. CAR HORNS – WHAT FOR?

4 JANUARY 2010 09:58

Critics of marketing and advertising often accuse us of creating 'noise' and 'clutter' (unless we tell them about something they want or find useful).

But there is one communications tool which, to my knowledge, has never been commercialised – but does make a noise. In fact, it exists to make a noise.

It is the horn of your car.

And, for some time, the question I have been asking myself is whether or not the intrusion, and occasional offence, of the noise made by car horns is disproportionate to the consumer benefit it generates?

I live in a 'normal' London street of 'normal' terraced houses. And I have come to learn what people are saying when they use their car horns. I've got the language.

There is the very early in the morning noise which is two short toot-toots, just like that. Toot-toot. This is the 5am cab that has come to pick up the guy with the Porsche three doors down to tell him 'I am here to take you to the airport'. Toot-toot. (Getting out of the car and ringing Mr Big's doorbell does not seem to be an option).

Ok, I know this is one important guy but, just because he needs to be up early, do all of us who live nearby have to wake up too?

Then, because my road has been conveniently designed to allow two cars to only just not-be-able-to-pass each other, one car has to pull in to allow the oncoming car through. By definition, it tends to be the case that this situation is more prevailing with the 4x4 status-symbol vehicle than the smaller, more street-friendly models (some of which are quite smart).

If there is nowhere to pull in, and both cars have committed to the road, they meet in the middle, realise one of them is going to reverse all the way back down again, know for a fact that it is the other idiot who

12.3. CAR HORNS – WHAT FOR?

should do this and – just to make their case more compelling – emit the much angrier, longer and louder 'TOOOOOOOT. This is the 'I got here first and I ain't moving' message.

It can happen at any time, day or night, and it means that all of us who live nearby, some of whom might be ill or have had a sleepless night with a new baby, have to wake up. And then, having been woken up by the first 'tooooot', we get the equally loud responding 'tooooot' – leading to a series of tooooooting ripostes of varying length and frequency of response.

Sometimes, one of the drivers gets out of his or her car and shouts loudly at the other driver through the closed window and, by now, locked door of the opponent. My theory is that this person is the loser. The physical act of getting out of the car, the delivery of a voluminous volley of verbal abuse, the stomping retreat and the loudest possible slamming of the car door on re-entry is actually the final gesture of submission leading to an inevitable, angry reversal of that driver's position.

If this happens in the middle of the day, and you are wide awake, this can all be quite entertaining and even lead to a shrug and a seen-it-all-before wave to your neighbour in the house over the road. Oh what fun!

But, if it is in the middle of the day, and you have had a bad night's sleep because of that baby again or you are ill or you are jet-lagged Mr Big, this is a hell of an intrusion and extremely annoying.

Round here, these are just two of the most common uses of the car horn medium.

But, from what I have heard, the absolutely most common use of the car horn is the one that substitutes those two short words, the second of which is 'off'. This is the long, loud 'TOOOOT-TOOOOT-TOOOOT'.

Someone has pulled out or changed lanes or merely even slowed down to let someone else in. Clearly, this absolutely deserves the full shot-gun volley of horny abuse and everyone – resident, pedestrian, mild mannered pensioner at the bus stop – yes, all of us have to know that one driver is telling another that he or she is a tooting moron and should toot off.

So why do we have these car horns?

Yes, I know that on country lanes, you need to let someone know you are approaching a corner. But how often does that happen?

Yes, I know that at town traffic lights, you have to alert the person who has not noticed the light ahead of you has gone green. But how do you know they are going to hear you? For all you know, they could be listening to loud garage music or be on the phone. These days, however loud you toot, how do you know your noisesome message will be heard?

Until recently, I thought my horn-aversion was a strictly personal foible.

But then, late last year, I had to catch one of those Mr Big early morning flights to a meeting in Vienna. And guess what? As we approached the centre of this old and beautiful city, we passed a road sign that had a picture of a bugle-looking thing with a red line across it.

I turned to the cab driver (for it was he) and asked "what does that sign mean?".

"It means you cannot use your car horn", he said.

"What, not at all?" I retorted, amazed and in hope.

"Not in the centre of the City of Vienna".

Oh joy! Oh wonder! Oh Christmas! Oh the Sound of Music!

So there you go. If they can do it in Vienna, why can't they do it here? Shall we launch a Campaign? You can sign up here.

Otherwise, why not join me in my New Year's Resolution never to use my horn unless absolutely necessary – and certainly never in anger?

Toot-toot.

12.4. Please don't blow that whistle!

10 June 2010 22:48

At what point does impact become intrusion?

Whistleblowing is a special interest of mine. I have personal experience of it. I support and applaud the work of the charity 'Public Concern at Work' which helps whistleblowers act in the public interest.

Much to their credit, PCAW pioneered the Public Interest Disclosure Act and drove it through Parliament.

So I was delighted to learn that, yet again, the Tories have taken one of my recommendations on board and that yesterday (9 June 2010), in his Oral Statement to the House of Commons, Health Secretary Andrew Lansley said:

"I can announce today that we are going to give teeth to the current safeguards for whistleblowers in the Public Interest Disclosure Act by reinforcing the NHS Constitution to make clear the rights and responsibilities of NHS staff and their employers in respect of whistleblowing".

However, my joyful enthusiasm and support for this announcement was tempered by something which suddenly made me very bad-tempered indeed:

Also yesterday (yes, the same day!) at the check-out counter of a reputable High Street store whose initials are M&S, I noticed that among the 'official England product' merchandise on offer is a red-ribboned chrome whistle.

I think, by now, most of us have worked out that the World Cup is upon us.

And I am delighted that it may provide one of the rare occasions where the English people can unite as one in support of our team. Convergence at last!

And I have no objection to public displays of support that will play their part in this convergence.

Key rings? Fine, though not essential.

T-shirts? OK too, though not too heavy on the belly please.

Flagging down cars? If you must.

But what possible contribution will be made by the blowing of these loathsome whistles whose sole planetary existence is to attract attention by making a noise?

Among all the merchandise that has been produced, WHO ON EARTH is the marketing person who approved this particular media channel? And which buyers of which reputable High Street stores have agreed to stock them?

What will these 'official' whistles – most likely blown by drunken football fans late at night on their way back from the pub – add to our enjoyment of this wonderfully convergent event?

Let me tell you, if I hear so much as a whisper from just ONE of these whistles, I for one am going to blow my top.

12.5. Do You Brighten the Space You Occupy?

23 August 2012 09:06

This summer I have been listening to the audiobook *'Life Beyond Measure'* written and read by Sidney Poitier although, when I say 'read', I should really say 'performed' so brilliant is Poitier's delivery.

Good actors have a wonderful talent of bringing the written word to life which is why I prefer to listen to, rather than read, books of this genre. Leslie Phillips' autobiography 'Hello' was infinitely better in the listening than the reading. Who can say 'hello' like Leslie Phillips let alone read 'The Owl and the Pussycat' by Edward Lear as he does?

Why Sidney Poitier? Well, he is from The Bahamas, a place I fell in love with several years ago, so I wanted to find out more about his life.

And what a life! Poitier's early years were spent in a tiny paradise called Cat Island.

So unspoilt was his childhood that he had not seen himself in a mirror until he moved to Nassau when he was ten.

He had no idea what he looked like. What torture for an actor!

In his teens, Poitier moved to America and, in 1963, won the Academy Award for Best Actor leaving him, today, as the oldest living recipient of that Oscar.

Poitier's book is written in the form of letters to his great-granddaughter. If a little sentimental at times, I think we can forgive that to an old man in his eighties.

He did use one sentence that lingers in the mind. Describing his half-sister Maude, he said 'she brightens the space she occupies'. Isn't that great?

I hope, one day, people will say I brighten the space I occupy.

How about you?

Do you brighten the space you occupy?

13

APPENDIX – BLOWING THE WHISTLE

13.1. Whistleblowers – Brave Heroes or Social Outcasts?

24 May 2012 09:02

The word 'whistleblower' has re-entered my life. I hate this word with a passion.

In the school playground, whistleblowing is called 'sneaking'. As a sneak, you are the person who has reported the misbehaviour of your schoolmates to the teachers. You cannot be trusted. You have behaved in a furtive, underhand way. You are left isolated, alone and friendless (every child's worst nightmare). You are contemptible.

In the criminal world, you are a 'snitch' or 'grass' (derived from 'snake in the grass'). You have reported the criminal activities of others to the police. You are an informant. And you are in grave danger. In retaliation, you risk being kneecapped, 'tarred and feathered' or killed. You are worse than contemptible. You could be dead.

But, in the wider world between the school playground and the criminal underground, isn't 'whistleblowing' a good thing?

For reasons I will come to later, whistleblowing is an aspect of human behaviour that is of particular interest to me. I like to learn about people who have been placed in a dilemma where their social conscience has been challenged to the extent they feel forced to, it says here, 'make public exposure of corruption or wrongdoing'.

In February, I read the obituary of an American rocket engineer called Roger Boisjoly 'whose warnings of catastrophe on the eve of the Challenger disaster went unheeded'.

Working for the company that made the booster rockets for the Challenger Space Shuttle, Boisjoly spotted a design fault that he investigated and reported to his company and NASA. The problem was that in cold temperatures the rubber sealing rings stiffened and became more likely to fail. 'The result', he warned, 'could be a catastrophe of the highest order'.

His findings were ignored. Shortly after take-off, the spacecraft exploded killing all seven crew members.

Then - and this is the social dynamic I hate – get this:

'In the days, months and years after the Challenger disaster, Boisjoly experienced intense feelings of guilt and depression. Recovery was not helped by the fact that many in the business he loved rejected him as an unwelcome whistle-blower.'

Isn't that dreadful?

What did Roger Boisjoly do wrong? Why did he feel 'guilt and depression'? Why was he 'rejected'?

I take a completely contrary view. I would like to declare that I admire and honour Roger Boisjoly. I had not heard of him until I read his obituary but, to me, Roger Boisjoly is a hero. May he rest in peace.

Whistleblowing also occurs in business. The lead story in the March issue of Management Today featured Michael Woodford, 'Britain's highest profile whistleblower', who was 'sacked as Chief Executive by the Olympus board for refusing to keep quiet about hundreds of millions of dollars of corrupt payments by the high-tech opticals maker'.

But, again, get this:

'And what of Woodford himself? A whistleblower's future is often a difficult and lonely one. Ejected from one pack, Woodford is now a lone wolf in his Thames lair. He has been to head-hunters, but it would be a bold gamble for a big corporation to hire him for a senior management role. It would probably worry that such a highly principled individual, however talented and cash generating, would prove a source of trouble.'

Isn't that dreadful?

And why am I, Hugh Salmon, so interested in the subject of whistleblowing? Why do I feel so strongly? Why do I get so emotional?

It is because, as long ago as October 1998, I featured in a lead story about whistleblowing in the very same magazine, Management Today. Please do not think I am trying to paint myself as a hero – frankly, in my case, I didn't think I had much option.

It seems, from Michael Woodford's case, that in the last thirteen years (despite the best efforts of a worthy charity called Public Concern at Work), nothing has changed.

And this makes me really angry.

13.1. WHISTLEBLOWERS – BRAVE HEROES OR SOCIAL OUTCASTS?

As I have discussed before, the biggest challenge we face in the world today is how to make capitalism work for the good of society as a whole.

Surely, in this day and age, if whistleblowers expose financial wrongdoing, they should be encouraged not rejected, welcomed not isolated, applauded not reviled?

It might be that we need a more positive word than 'whistleblower'.

How about 'honest broker'?

'UK: The Whistle blower's dilemma' by Matthew Lynn
Management Today, 1st October 1998.

13.2. THE WHISTLEBLOWER'S DILEMMA – WHAT WOULD YOU DO?

31 May 2012 22:07

Further to my last post on whistleblowing, and my own experience thereof, sometimes I get asked to conduct seminars and workgroups on 'Integrity in Business'.

The most rewarding sessions are when I place the participants into a position where the thin grey line between their moral integrity and financial or career ambitions is challenged.

Let's take a hypothetical example:

1. You own and manage a strategic marketing consultancy. You are successful but not rich. You have personal overheads – mortgage, loans, car, children. You know how it is.

2. You are contacted by a long-standing business contact (the 'Contact') who specialises in mergers and acquisitions (M&A) and company turnarounds.

3. He has a client (the 'Client') who owns a small, provincial UK engineering company that is in financial trouble.

On behalf of the Client, your Contact proposes to place the company into administration and then buy it back, restructure the business and re-launch it into an important market, which is where he has asked you to get involved.

The factory and offices are too far for you or your Contact to travel each day so the Client agrees to fund the use of an apartment nearby. This is where you and your Contact will base yourselves during the week while you rescue, redefine and re-launch this business.

But there is a sting. Because the Client company has gone into administration, and is now trading as a new business under a new name, no estate agent will trust the new company with the lease of the apartment.

13.2. THE WHISTLEBLOWER'S DILEMMA – WHAT WOULD YOU DO?

So, in good faith but perhaps rather naïvely, you agree to rent the flat and buy the furniture – subject to an agreement with the Client that you will be reimbursed in full from the revenue generated by the new company.

Your Contact says he knows a cheap furniture store near where he lives and you agree that he will choose all the furniture required and you will pay for it.

The invoice for the furniture arrives. It totals £5,250. You pay it.

However, as an experienced business professional, there is something about the invoice that does not seem right; there is a name but no address; there is no invoice number and, this is the strangest thing, the furniture you have bought and paid for is not specified item by item, piece by piece, price by price. You smell a rat.

So you call the accounts department at the furniture store and they agree to send you the invoices for the furniture bought and paid for by you.

When you receive these invoices you realise, with disappointment and no little anger, that the furniture for the apartment you have rented has not cost the sum you have paid for it.

In fact, it is revealed that the furniture you have bought and paid for can be neatly divided into two separate deliveries:

1. The furniture that has been delivered to the apartment you have rented near the factory. This consists of an armchair, a sofa, a nest of side tables, two beds, four chests of drawers, a dining table and four dining chairs. The cost of this delivery is £3,100.

2. A separate order which has been delivered to an address in the Contact's wife's name and over 100 miles from the Client business. This consists of a two-seater sofa, a three-seater sofa, a nest of side tables, a lamp table, a wardrobe, two chests of drawers, an extending dining table and six dining chairs. The cost of this delivery is £2,150.

As you can see, the total cost of these two deliveries comes to £5,250.

You now face the whistleblower's dilemma.

From now on, whatever you do, all future actions are underpinned by a racing certainty that any trust you may have had in your Contact has been greedily betrayed.

1. Is this theft?
2. Do you tell your Client?

3. Do you report it to the Police?

4. Do you confront your Contact and demand your money back, after which all will be forgiven? If so, will you be able to look your Contact in the eye again, especially while sharing the apartment you have agreed to share with the furniture you have bought and paid for?

5. Do you do nothing, take it on the chin and, desirous of this revenue stream, carry on regardless, avoiding the need to involve the Client (or the Police) but hoping that the ongoing revenue from the Client will make up for your financial loss in the long run?

6. Or is there another option which, confused and alone, you have failed to consider?

This is the whistleblower's dilemma.

What would you do?

13.3. WHISTLEBLOWING – A CALL FOR NEW LEGISLATION

7 JUNE 2012 08:51

On 24 May, when I posted the first of this trilogy on whistleblowing, I referred to a front page article in Management Today on Michael Woodford, 'the British chief executive who blew the whistle on a $1.7bn (£1bn) corporate fraud at Japanese electronics giant Olympus'.

Little did I know that now, only two weeks later, The Telegraph would report that:

'Woodford has brokered an out-of-court deal with the company over his sacking, believed to involve a multi-million pound payout … At a five-minute hearing yesterday (28 May), Mr Woodford's lawyer Thomas Linden QC said that the two sides had reached an 'agreement' to be rubber-stamped by Olympus's board on June 8. Outside the tribunal, Mr Woodford said he could 'give no guidance' on reports he had received an eight-figure settlement … 'I'm not at liberty, under the terms of the agreement, to go into any detail,' he said. 'But I genuinely hope, in the interests of Olympus, it helps them go forward and also for my own life and that of my family [to go forward]. Hopefully today is a closure, a line has been drawn. The company can move on and I can.'

What announcement will be made after 8 June? Will all the allegations of fraud that Woodward has made be admitted to be true? Will the perpetrators be identified? Will they be punished? Or will the whole thing be washed up in some bland public statement?

Obviously, we do not know. I fear, after 8 June, that we may still not know.

And this – the fact that we may never know – is what worries me and leads me to the point I want to make. For I do hope that, by the terms of this agreement, Olympus will not be able to:

i) 'cover up' the full details of the wrongdoings reported by Woodford;

ii) 'protect' the identities of the individuals who perpetrated the 'fraud' (saving them from prosecution and punishment for what may or may not have been criminal activity).

What I do know is that, in my own case against Lintas (reported by Management Today in 1998), by settling out of court, Interpublic were able to:

i) deny me the chance to reveal in Court the full evidence I had gathered against the individual managers involved (which I very much wanted to do);

ii) continue to employ them for many years afterwards (rather than face criminal prosecution).

So why did I settle? Good question. I am afraid you will have to believe me when I say that, such is the legal system by which we are bound, I was left with no option. However, I did refuse to sign a 'gagging' clause, which is why I am at liberty to discuss the case now.

So, for the purposes of the case I want to make in this post, let's return to the hypothetical case history discussed in my last post.

Given that there was an outstanding fee involved, it would be no surprise if the Client were to insist that an agreement 'to settle all outstanding claims' would be conditional on you (the Consultant) agreeing to 'gagging' clauses along the following lines:

'The Consultant (you) agrees and undertakes to the Companies and the Directors not to:

i) Make or publish any statement to a third party concerning this Agreement, the dispute settled by it or the circumstances surrounding the termination of the Consultant's involvement in the Companies;

ii) Make or publish any derogatory or disparaging statement or do anything in relation to the Companies, the Directors and any employees of or consultants to the Companies which is intended to or which might be expected to damage or lower their respective reputations'.

Now, this is what I object to.

Why should any company be able to 'gag' a whistleblower to protect their reputations?

The human insight I would make, based on my own painful experience, is that it is the whistleblower – the honest broker who stands up for what he or she thinks is the right thing to do whatever the cost of this stance to their own career or financial interests – who is blamed for being the trouble maker (not the perpetrators of the fraud).

13.3. WHISTLEBLOWING – A CALL FOR NEW LEGISLATION

Why is this?

It is my very strong opinion that it should be against the law – a criminal offence – for any company, or the directors of any company and even their lawyers, to draw up 'agreements' whereby paying money to a whistleblower is made subject to that person agreeing not to reveal the financial wrongdoing or fraud he or she has unwillingly discovered.

This is the classic corporate 'cover up'. And far too much of it goes on in business today.

In this vital debate we are having about how capitalism can work for the good of society as a whole, how can business people be allowed to 'cover up' fraud in this way?

It is an absolute disgrace, of which everyone in business should be thoroughly ashamed.

Fraud is fraud. Stealing is stealing. Theft is theft.

Too many businesses get away with it.

And it is so, so wrong.

ACKNOWLEDGEMENTS

9 JANUARY 2015

I would like to thank all my school teachers for everything you did for me. You dedicated your lives to improving the lives of others and are a noble breed. Especially the late, great Jim Ramage and Hugh Atkins who recognised and developed any writing skills I might have.

I have many people to thank:

In the University of Life, Peter Hunt was a shining star then and forever.

Clive Aldred recruited me twice: for Ogilvy & Mather London in 1979 and then O&M Thailand in 1988. Robert Deighton recruited me twice too: for Foote, Cone & Belding and then Kirkwoods which became Deighton & Mullen. Thank you, gentlemen.

For the glory days of SFX, I must recognise the heroic support of the late Derek Ralston, Chris Lever, Alison Cruikshank, Tony Monteuuis, the great Max Bell and countless others.

At O&M Thailand, I would like to thank everyone in the Bangkok office while I was there, especially Simon Bolton for our special friendship then and since.

With my lawyer, the late John Lloyd, we stood up and fought the might of Interpublic, a publicly quoted company in New York. We beat the crooked bastards! Without John, I could never have done it. I will always be grateful.

At The Salmon Agency, Anthony Stileman and Samantha Etheridge had special faith in me. And thanks to all the others who came on board, especially my long-standing client The Bahamas Tourist Office. What a country! What a people!

Through sport, I have learnt so much about life:

In cricket, I must thank all my friends in all the clubs I played for, especially the legend that is Chris Potter and my fellow tourists in Sri Lanka 1982-83, South Africa 1983-84 and Australia 1984-85.

ACKNOWLEDGEMENTS

In rugby, special thanks to my best man Robin Gale who shared an unforgettable experience supporting England in New Zealand in 1985. Plus all who came on that extraordinary tour to Kenya in 1988. Hakuna Matata! And the OWRFC, of course. Special memories, too, of Greg Stitcher who died in that horrible game in April 1993. You changed my life, Greg.

Caroline D'Auria gave me remarkable strength, wisdom and support in the 2010 General Election campaign in Battersea. What a lady. We helped achieve the building of a badly needed new secondary school in our borough. Don't float – vote!

Lovereading.co.uk has been an interesting journey in which, thirty years after we attended the FCB Management Course in Chicago in 1985, Nick West has shown extraordinary friendship at times when I have most needed a friend.

There have been many doctors and nurses who have treated and tended my old back and helped me cope with constant, chronic pain. You are a noble breed too.

Finally, of course, Ricki, Kris, Nik and Becki of whom I am so proud. What a team. What a family!

Time for the next chapter, eh?